THE
ART OF
INDUSTRY

Tom Bochsler, Photographer

Master of Photographic Arts (Canada)
Craftsman Photographer, USA
Fellow, Professional Photographers of Ontario

"Photography is a window to history, one must open the window to appreciate its value."

Tom Bochsler, 2006

Published by:
From the Heart Publishing
119 Duncairn Crescent
Hamilton, Ontario, Canada L9C 6E9
t: 905 630-2556
w: www.fromtheheart.ca

Library and Archives Canada / Bibliotheque & Archives Canada
ISBN 978-0-9685879-7-3

All Photographs by: Tom Bochsler, Copyright © 2010.

TEXT BY: Tom Bochsler
PHOTOGRAPHY: Tom Bochsler
TEXT EDITOR: Mark Zelinski
TEXT EDITING: Gerry Ormond, Doreen Bochsler, Bob Chambers
BOOK DESIGN: Peter M. Bochsler
PUBLISHER: From the Heart Publishing, Mark Zelinski
SCANS AND PROOFING: Bochsler Creative Solutions, Burlington, ON
PRINTED BY: Paramount Printing Co. Ltd., Hong Kong

For more information about the work of Tom Bochsler
e: tbplbook@gmail.com
w: bpimaging.com

Front Cover:
Boiler Manufacturing
Foster Wheeler, 1973
St. Catherines, Ontario

Dedicated to my wife Doreen
and our children Bernadette, Cindy (Don), Jean-Pierre (Debbi), Peter & Marianne,
and grand children Brandon, Caitlin, Cassie, Nairn, Rachel, Jesse, Jeremy,
Daniel, Lucas & Graeme.

As hard as one works, there has to be time for family.

Mark Zelinski

I n this new millennium of rapid change and the meteoric advance in information technology, it easy to forget our history. "The Art of Industry" brings focus to the rich industrial and cultural heritage of the great province of Ontario and beyond, over a defining 50 year period.

Through the exquisite photography of Tom Bochsler, we can now explore the industry, lifestyle, celebrities and businesses of the latter half of the 20th Century as it relates to our constantly evolving community. This nostalgic collection should prove to be a useful and enlightening document of how our resources and directions in the past, have shaped the present.

THE HONOURABLE LINCOLN M. ALEXANDER,
P.C., C.C., K. ST.J., O. ONT., Q.C.

**George
Hunter
Photography**

A good photographer is not only an artist, he is a historian.
This is especially true when it portrays entities created by man.

Painters, sculptors, architects and other artists' creations occur firstly in their
mind's eye. Photographers use their skills to capture the beauty of nature and
to produce images of man's creations in a dramatic fashion that will make them
memorable. These images will withstand the test of time long after the subjects
themselves may have disappeared.

For over five decades in his professional career, Tom Bochsler has used the key
elements of lighting, design and creativity to turn mundane industrial interiors,
activities and events into bright, dynamic pieces of art. Working with corporate and
governmental clients, Tom has created a wealth of photographic images which are
not only pieces of true art, but are also a historical record of industry in Hamilton,
throughout Ontario, and across Canada, for well over half a century.

In my experience in photography for seven decades, I have seen no better industrial
work than Tom's. I take great pleasure in congratulating him on his diversified
efforts to record Canadian history in a style that communicates through photography.

GEORGE HUNTER
RCA

Introduction

Photography appeals to me in many different ways. Whether it is the detail, mood and atmospherics created by black and white images or the rainbow mosaic of full, saturated colour, photography continues to fascinate me. Whatever the content, photography tells a story. And we are all drawn to the story, the photographer and the viewers, curious to have reflected back to us the light and the shape of a captured moment.

From my early years as a photographer, as I honed my craft, my initial priority was to develop my technical expertise. To achieve this, through careful observation, experimentation and practice, I became quite fluent and adept with the medium of photography. Lighting, exposure and technical mastery became second nature to me. Fortunately, these skills would play an increasingly crucial role in my freelance career, as I found myself on assignment in a variety of sometimes difficult locations and often challenging environments. As a result, I discovered to my (and my clients') relief that I could surmount the technical hurdles in most situations. This allowed me to concentrate on telling the story at hand, creatively and dramatically.

I always enjoyed being on assignment and challenged by the subject matter. Often, it was the work behind the shot that compelled me. The technical hurdles that I encountered on site, without the comfort of a studio with everything readily at hand, were what engaged me most. I always had to determine what I'd need beforehand and try to anticipate any problems. I became a kind of photographic choreographer, often orchestrating the movement of men, mammoth machinery, dust choked environments and careful lighting to achieve just the right balance of aesthetics and documentary record. On occasion, it was simply serendipity - being at the right place at the right time and capturing that moment.

I feel that one of the singular reasons for any success I have enjoyed as a commercial industrial photographer, is that I approached each assignment without a preconceived bias. I always tried to be as open to the subject matter as I could be. I would try to bring a fresh viewpoint, a creative outlook and strive for the quintessential image. I discovered that this approach paid dividends in the form of repeat business and more clients receptive to my vision and high standards.

Beginning with the artistry of my stone mason father Thomas, I have been part of a unique photographic family. My oldest brother Joseph introduced me to photography in 1950, then my younger brother Albert joined in. Each of us has a son who has followed in a career of photography — Joseph's son Joe, Albert's son Mark and my son Jean Pierre.

My career has been full of a variety of interesting people and things. I have photographed Hollywood stars and giant turbines and nuclear power plants; disasters and weddings, advertising campaigns and news, steel mills and athletes. Through it all, I have always tried to find the drama and the interest in the scene and to convey what I saw with just a little insight, inspiration and dedication. I trust that this series of images will serve as a window on a way of life which now seems to have slipped away forever.

TOM BOCHSLER
MPA, CPA, FPPO

1

Steel making, storms
& Studebakers

August 26, 1957
A COUPLE OF ASSES
Personal Work

BRANTFORD, ONTARIO
Early in my career, I spent my days shooting, and developing and printing at night.

It wasn't long before I learned of the unwritten newspaper edict, "If you don' t come back with the picture the editor requested, don't bother to come back at all. Save the embarrassment".

George Hunter, Location photographer

Flash bulbs and Speed Graphics cameras were the norm for press and event photography.

January 25, 1958

**GIBSON BAKERY
HOME DELIVERY**

HAMILTON, ONTARIO

This brings back memories of some real Canadian Winters. Knowing every stop on the route, the old-fashioned horse-drawn wagon always persevered, in conditions where cars had difficulty maneuvering. From time to time I made it a point to freeze a moment in history.

February 22, 1960

FOUNDRY MAN
International Harvester Co. Ltd.

HAMILTON, ONTARIO
Shown here, a foundry worker pours
molten steel into a ladle from an electric
furnace. The steel was then formed in
small batch forgings, and manufactured
into plough shears and other components
of farm machinery.

November 25, 1950

VAN WAGNER BEACH ROAD WASHOUT
Storm scene and sandbagging

HAMILTON, ONTARIO
The many newspaper photo assignments that I covered often contained an element of the unexpected. When Lake Ontario kicked up its version of a 'big one' the storm completely washed out the only road along the lake in east Hamilton. With my trusty 4x5 Speed Graphic, I found a vantage point on the roof of one of the cottages to record the sandbagging crew and area volunteers who joined the fold in less than pleasant weather.

July 24, 1963

SATCHMO
900 CHML Radio

HAMILTON, ONTARIO
Louis (Louie) Armstrong, with his 'trade
mark smile', was the most famous
musician in the history of jazz. When he
performed at Burlington's venerable
Brant Inn, Radio CHML's R.O. Horning
Jr. was there for the interview.

November 10, 1956

**LAUNCHING
A NEW TRANSLUX SIGN**
CKOC Radio media event

HAMILTON, ONTARIO
From a vantage point on the second
floor of the Hamilton Spectator office
building I photographed the activity,
publicity and hype for Loblaws' new
Translux message reader sign in
downtown Hamilton. The main street
had been partially blocked off for the
Friday night shopping crowd.

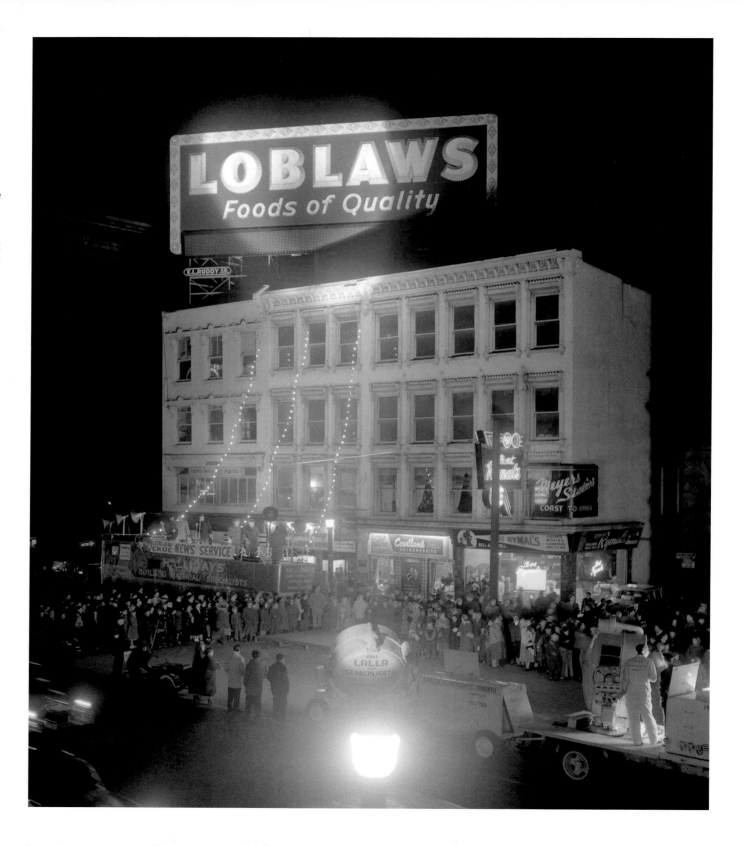

August 26, 1957

EARLY TIMES
Tom with donkeys

BRANTFORD, ONTARIO

In the late fifties, after photographing some of the new model black & white television sets at the Westinghouse manufacturing plant in Brantford, public relations executive Mike Mackrory and I were driving back to Hamilton. We noticed a couple of donkeys in a farmer's field, and decided that it would be neat to make some fun photographs. I've used these many times in talks about my early trials in photography.

January 12, 1958

COOTES PARADISE
Personal work

HAMILTON, ONTARIO

A Sunday afternoon family drive on a cold winter day revealed how many people in the Hamilton/Dundas/ Burlington area enjoy our natural recreation spots.
Being fairly new in my own business, I saw an opportunity to make an interesting photograph for The Hamilton Spectator. I developed the film and print that Sunday evening and took it to the editor for possible use. The next day, it was published.
Fifty years later it was reprinted by The Spec in Paul Wilson's 'Streetbeat'.

September 6, 1958
CAT CRACKER
Shell Oil Refinery

CLARKSON, ONTARIO
Being part of a professional association provides opportunities to be tuned in to the latest equipment, styles, techniques - and sometimes even business savvy. The Shell Oil Refinery invited the 20 plus members from of the Commercial & Press Photographers Association of Canada to visit the plant. Any resulting photographs could then be submitted for a competition. I won the contest and a $20.00 prize for this photograph of the 'cat cracker', a catalytic processor to convert oil to a host of products. The company then wanted exclusive use of the negative. My negotiating skills were not great, and I was so pleased to have won my first photographic competition that no further money changed hands.

November 7, 1958

LESTER B. PEARSON'S VISIT TO WESTINGHOUSE
Westinghouse Canada

HAMILTON, ONTARIO
As an industrial/public relations photographer I've had the opportunity to experience a wide range of locations, events and celebrated people. When Lester B. Pearson came for a tour of the Westinghouse motor generator division in Hamilton, I positioned him with company executives to give scale to the motor frame.

L-R James Kerr, vice president of Westinghouse, Mr. Lester B. Pearson (future Prime Minister of Canada), H.H. Rogge, President of Westinghouse Canada and future Westinghouse president, George Wilcox.

April 19, 1960

'WE STAND ON GUARD FOR THEE'
Ontario Attorney General Department

HAMILTON, ONTARIO
One of my earliest major projects with Russell T. Kelley Advertising was to photograph a complete series of services within the responsibility of the Ontario Attorney General's office. Public safety, bicycle safety, highway rules and restrictions, school bus regulations were among the themes of the images created to enhance police perception and community relations. Sgt. Ed Selinski of the Hamilton City Police was the key subject in many of the photos. Forty six years later (in 2006) Sgt. Ed cut the ribbon for an exhibition of my industrial images at the Art Gallery of Hamilton.

October 6, 1960 & January 26, 1961

MAIN STREET JAMBOREE
CHCH-TV

HAMILTON, ONTARIO

In the early 1950's I traveled to locations across Ontario to photograph the very popular CHML Main Street Jamboree and their performers. This country music group invited Nashville Stars as guests to fan-filled community and high school auditoriums. When CHCH-TV went on the air, CHML owner Ken Soble brought the group to television.

Comedy singer/writers Homer & Jethro entertained with the Jamboree regulars. I was particularly impressed to see real professionals perform on and off camera. The small studio audience always got more than they expected.

October 6, 1960

**JOHNNY CASH
ON MAIN STREET JAMBOREE**
CHCH-TV

HAMILTON, ONTARIO
In his youth Johnny Cash was one of
the early country western stars to visit
CHCH-TV's Main Street Jamboree,
shown here with host Bill Long.
Twenty years later I had the chance to
photograph Johnny Cash again, as part
of a Canada Trust promotion for the
Johnny Cash Bank machine.

May 20, 1965

TINY TALENT TIME
CHCH-TV

HAMILTON, ONTARIO

Another 'kids' show was 'Tiny Talent Time' hosted by Bil Lawrence. Bil interviewed these great little entertainers. A live television presentation, no video tape for edits. One of the goals of CHCH-TV was to offer a venue for the community participation.

March 12, 1962

ROMPER ROOM
CHCH-TV

HAMILTON, ONTARIO

Miss Lois was the teacher for the Romper Room class every week. The children were taught and entertained. Our 6 year old daughter Bernadette was in one of the classes. Miss Lois asked her why she was wrapping some cookies in a serviette. She replied that she wanted to take some home for her little sister Cindy.

July 27, 1960

SKYWAY BRIDGE
Westinghouse Canada

BURLINGTON, ONTARIO

Westinghouse created the lighting for the newly constructed Skyway Bridge and needed to show the results of their product in use. I selected a vantage point of the Hamilton Bay link to Lake Ontario, and with the help of an assistant we directed flash bulbs into the trees to highlight the trees. The Ontario Department of Highways liked the shot so much they ordered a three metre-wide print for the Canadian National Exhibition. The Minister of Highways, Mr. Fred Cass, said it was the best shot he had seen of the bridge.

NURSERY

NURSES ON DUTY
St. Joseph's Hospital

HAMILTON, ONTARIO
I must have made an impression with PR photography for The Hamilton Spectator's Kingsley Brown. The senior writer at The Spec, made the recommendation for this assignment to Joseph M. Pigott, president of Pigott Construction and chairman of the fundraising for St. Joseph's Hospital expansion campaign.

A Publicity photography can be a great venue to portray human interest and candid scenes. Pretty student nurses with newborns under the charge of Sister Ursula made a good introduction to the maternity wing.

B For someone who is squeamish about things medical, I soon learned to overcome my discomfort and get on with the job. I wore a gown in the OR, using flash equipment that would not ignite oxygen used in the operation, and did my best to produce an image that best described the procedures.

C Providing bottles for several daily feedings is a major undertaking in the maternity section.

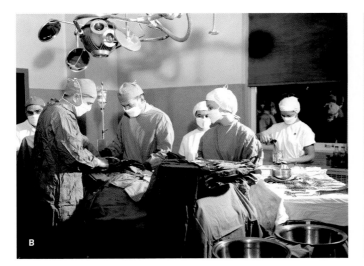

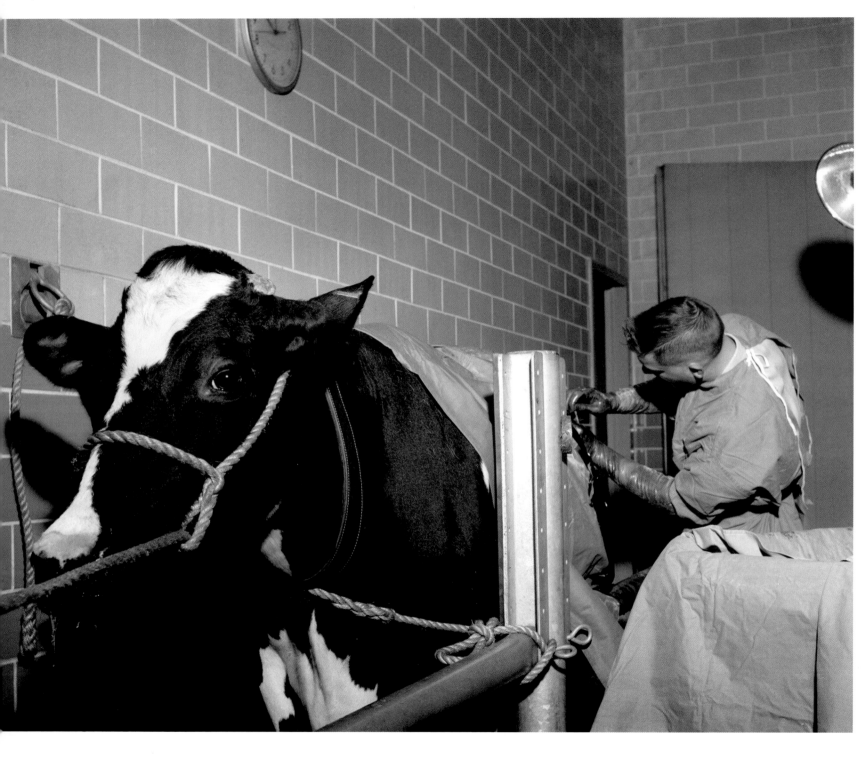

February 6, 1961

TOUR OF OPERATING ROOM
Ontario Veterinarian College

GUELPH, ONTARIO
As an active participant of the Professional Photographers Organization, I often toured the work places of fellow members. This image, taken at the Ontario Veterinary College facility in Guelph, was the winning image (prize $20.00) of a photo competition. It was selected because it conveyed the surgery in a gritty style.

June 21, 1962

NUCLEAR REACTOR
McMaster University

HAMILTON, ONTARIO
Through editorial/industrial photography I always tried to create a visual presentation in a dramatic and informative way. Over the years I shot feature photo stories of McMaster's diverse areas of learning (astronomy, chemistry, geography, arts, etc.) McMaster University was the first to have an on-campus teaching and research reactor in North America, bringing international attention to the university. Working in this environment was new to me, passing through an air-locking chamber and radiation checkpoints.

Dr. Harry Thode **(above)** was head of nuclear sciences and eventually president of McMaster University.

March 31, 1962

HANK SNOW & PATSY CLINE
900 CHML Radio

HAMILTON, ONTARIO

Country music stars that visited CHML included Patsy Cline, the famous singer who met an untimely death in a plane crash.

Hank Snow was a small man with a big voice, who reigned as a leading country singer for decades. Born in Nova Scotia, he spent most of his career in Nashville.

January 9, 1963

**QUALITY CONTROL
TURBINE SPINDLE**
Westinghouse Canada

HAMILTON, ONTARIO
Turbines were produced by
Westinghouse Canada in several
varieties for gas and steam power
applications. One application was to
provide the power to pump natural
gas from Alberta to Eastern Canada
through the Trans Canada Pipe Line.

Each design provided me with
photographic challenges. To effectively
publicize the company's products, the
resulting images had to be interesting
and reproduce well in newsprint. That's
where my abilities and techniques of
lighting and print quality were important.

It should be noted that many of my
older photographs show men working
without safety glasses. This wasn't
mandatory at the time but became a
rule in later years.

February 23, 1963

TURBINE ROTOR MACHINING
Westinghouse Canada

HAMILTON, ONTARIO
Since my first photograph, I've strived to make each image communicate the ordinary in a remarkable way. This photograph marks the turning point in my understanding of creative lighting in industry, and it happened by chance.

To portray this machinist working on a turbine component, I used several electronic flash lights to create effective lighting. The moment I was to make my exposure, the light nearest the camera dropped to the floor and stopped working. Without a replacement light I made my several exposures and discovered that this lighting treatment would create an exceptional three-dimensional photographic effect, sculpting the shape of the object. I have applied this style of lighting for over 50 years.

October 18, 1962

STEEL SLAB PROCESSING
Steel Company of Canada

HAMILTON, ONTARIO
Scarfing. Before I was assigned to photograph this, I had no idea of what it was. Scarfing is a stage in quality control of a steel slab when the worker cuts out obvious imperfections with an oxygen lance before it is reheated and rolled into steel plate or sheet products.

April 23, 1963

**JAYNE MANSFIELD'S
VISIT TO HAMILTON**
900 CHML Radio

HAMILTON, ONTARIO
Event photography is a category that
suggests something special. Having
movie star Jayne Mansfield visit
Hamilton was definitely an event for the
media. Because CHML Radio sponsored
her visit, as their photographer I was
able to make some pretty images. After
her untimely and tragic death a few
years later, I ghosted a second image of
her into this photo.

June 13, 1963

SMOTHERS BROTHERS
900 CHML Radio

HAMILTON, ONTARIO

The Perc Allen CHML Radio Show was livened up when the Smothers Brothers arrived. Some of the stars that I worked with were very friendly and some barely accommodated my posing directions. A few of the visiting personalities that I photographed include Igor Gouzenko (who wore a bag to disguise his identity), Spike Jones, Guy Lombardo, and Johnny Mathis, to name a few.

December 12, 1963

**GAS TURBINE ROTOR
QUALITY CONTROL**
Westinghouse Canada

HAMILTON, ONTARIO
Manufacturers are always interested
in projecting an image of quality. The
composition and lighting in this image
of a turbine assemblyman conveyed
this well. The darkened background
eliminated distracting elements in the
aging factory, making this shot ideal for
a wide distribution news release.

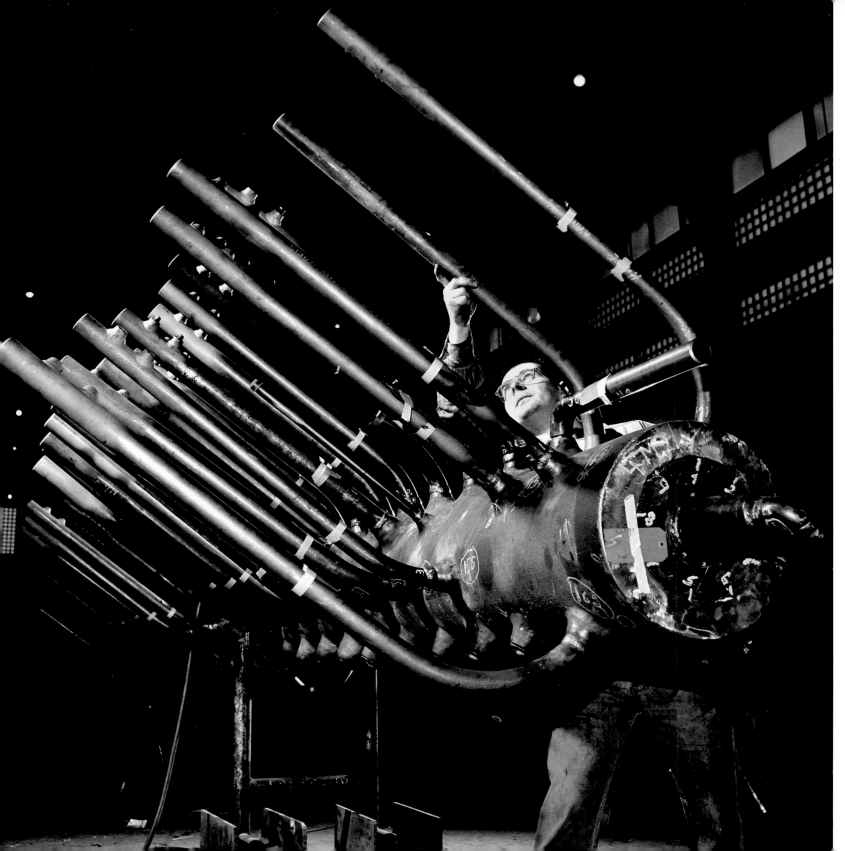

December 18, 1963

CANDU NUCLEAR MANIFOLD
Douglas Point Reactor
Atomic Energy of Canada

HAMILTON, ONTARIO
This is the first photograph that I made
for Atomic Energy of Canada (AECL) of
fabricating components for Canada's
first nuclear power reactor. The piping
manifold was one of many required
for water or steam distribution within
the reactor building. Upon first seeing
this equipment, I visualized a striking
impact potential with the right choice of
angle and lighting. This photograph was
used in national publicity, and began a
relationship that's lasted over 20 years,
involving hundreds of photographs in all
of the nuclear power plants in Canada.

January 8, 1965
READY FOR EXPORT
Studebaker Canada

HAMILTON, ONTARIO
In 1963, the last vestiges of the
Studebaker motorcar company struggled
to keep the brand going when Hamilton
was designated as their only auto
manufacturing centre. Here, a line
of new models are set up for export.
Unfortunately sales dropped and
Studebaker ceased operations in 1966.

September 25 ,1964

TRANSFORMER BUSHINGS
Westinghouse Canada

HAMILTON, ONTARIO
Westinghouse built some amazing equipment to transmit and convert electrical power. These conductors and transformer bushings were massive but had to be installed for testing while in the plant. As part of preparing the location, I always showed a tidy workplace which implied safe working conditions.

My vantage point was crucial in emphasizing these unusual transformer bushings. After testing has been completed the fabrication is disassembled for shipping.

July 30, 1971

TIGER CAT FOOTBALL
Hamilton Tiger Cat Football Club

HAMILTON, ONTARIO

For many years, I photographed the Tiger Cat players and team group shots for their publicity. It was a great relationship. Using a specially designed camera and wide-angle lens, I was able to illustrate the new stadium lighting manufactured by Westinghouse Canada.

October 19, 1964

**GLEN RICHARDSON
CURLING PRO**
Firestone Canada

HAMILTON, ONTARIO
With little information about the
assignment, I was asked on short
notice to photograph Glen Richardson,
Canada's curling champion in 1964.
With no previous knowledge of the
game I needed to learn fast. With the
capable assistance of a good art director
and Glen, I was able to produce a series
of "curling tips' photographs for a
booklet by Firestone.

April 8, 1965

**FORD MUSTANG
STAINLESS WHEEL COVERS**
Atlas Steels

Atlas Steels wanted to feature stainless steel wheel covers on the latest model Ford Mustang. As a location and background, we selected the mill area where the coils of stainless steel are actually prepared. The shot was set up at the lunch hour to avoid interruption to production.

April 21, 1965

TIRE PRODUCTION
Firestone Canada

HAMILTON, ONTARIO

Firestone tire building had several stages of on line quality control. Since this type of photography was generally used for press releases, I needed to give particular attention to design, reflections and lighting to ensure that the images reproduced well.

November 2, 1965

ST. LAWRENCE SEAWAY SHAFT
Bridge & Tank

HAMILTON, ONTARIO
The St. Lawrence Seaway development project brought considerable business to Hamilton's Bridge & Tank Company. Most of the components for lock gates and mechanisms were very large and took considerable skill and capability to produce. For ongoing publicity, I was frequently called into the plant to photograph equipment in a dramatic and informative way.

November 26, 1965

STATOR FRAME ASSEMBLY
Westinghouse

HAMILTON, ONTARIO
In my early career of industrial
photography, I made photographs to
involve the public in the work and
products of many companies. Whenever
possible, I included a technician to give
scale and to add a human element.
This large motor component had a
series of contact heads, which were
aligned before final assembly. In later
years, equipment was designed and
built to enclose much of the activity for
safety and environmental purposes.

February 21, 1966

**STEEL GIRDER
COMPUTERIZED STEEL CUTTING**
Bridge & Tank

HAMILTON, ONTARIO

Large engineered steel girder sections are required to build bridges, and it is the machinist's precise skills that made the job complete. The cutting table shown here cuts 2.5 cm steel plate into specific multiple patterns as defined by a programmed machine.

February 21, 1966

**HOT WATER TANK
PRODUCTION LINE**
Rheem Canada

HAMILTON, ONTARIO
For a series of annual report
photographs, I used the production
line and staged some hot water tanks
to create composition and hide messy
background areas. It was quite
important to a company's image to
exhibit good housekeeping in
manufacturing operations.

2
Bridges, bathtubs & beer tanks

January 10, 1967

IN PLANT MANUFACTURING
Bridge & Tank

HAMILTON, ONTARIO
To illustrate how equipment is built
or fabricated is what makes industrial
photography challenging. My job was to
graphically interpret industrial scenes
that convey excellence and precision in
safe, tidy work areas.

"Don't make me out to be an artist. I am an engineer. I am after the facts, only the facts. In many ways, unexpected results are what have most inspired my photography."

Harold Edgerton, inventor of the electronic flash

For more advanced commercial/ industrial/architectural photography, the specialized (old fashioned) view camera was a must.

February 21, 1966

**GRAIN HARVESTING
EQUIPMENT**
IH International Harvester

HAMILTON, ONTARIO
Companies like to emphasize their
dedication to producing quality
equipment. For the IH Annual Report
1965, specific activity needed to
be recorded to accommodate the
designer's layout and theme. Tungsten
lighting was used in combination with
the ambient light, and the subjects
remained motionless for the time
exposure of several seconds.

April 15, 1966

TRUCK DIVISION
International Harvester

HAMILTON, ONTARIO
The newest product from International
Harvester truck division was the
'Scout' (sport type vehicle). I made
arrangements with the Hamilton Parks
Department to shoot the truck with
models in one of the local parks. We set
the scene to show off-road use without
damaging the landscape.

April 15, 1966

**PLACING BRIDGE SECTION
BY FLOTATION**
Bridge & Tank

SEVERN BRIDGE, ONTARIO

When I arrived at the site north of Orillia, at 5:30am, I shot an innovative installation of a large highway bridge section by the use of flotation tanks which lifted the girder up and into place. Workplace knowledge and safety concerns were prime ingredients to make effective photographs in this environment.

May 17, 1966

**STEEL MILL BRIDGE CRANE
FINAL CHECK**
Bridge & Tank

HAMILTON, ONTARIO
Unlike most industrial and location photographers today, who usually work with assistants on large projects, I would tackle the most complex assignments with just the co-operation of plant staff. This was always great, especially when I made them aware of my goal.

This large capacity steel mill crane was almost ready to disassemble and ship. I chose the evening shift when fumes and noise from welding and machining would be minimal. After selecting my viewpoint from the crane cab above, I set up my tungsten lighting around, and even on top of, the crane itself. I instructed two workmen to be positioned and await my signal after I was back in the crane cab, which entailed several trips. Since the plant was relatively quiet, my instructions could be easily heard and the exposures with the 4x5 camera were made. The whole task took several hours and the photographs were widely used.

August 24, 1966

MULTIPLE REFLECTIONS
Atlas Steels

WELLAND, ONTARIO
Studio photography was not a specialty
in my early career, but when clients
presented a challenge it was rewarding
to provide an effective result. Atlas
Steels produced a variety of stainless
steels for architecture, products and
appliances. The image shown is created
from three curved sections of stainless
steel reflecting into each other.
I borrowed a small pitcher from
a gift shop to enhance the design,
depth and reflectivity.

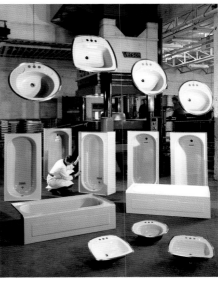

September 20, 1966

**TUB & SINK PRODUCT
FINISHING LINE**
Slater Industries

CAMBRIDGE, ONTARIO

Annual report photography is one of the more challenging aspects of visual communication. In some applications, several photographs may be used to describe the company, its people, products, capital expenditures etc. In an annual report, one facet must describe a complete division or department.

The grouping of tubs and sinks was conceived to show variety and colours available.

September 14, 1977

LARGE VESSEL
Bridge & Tank Company

HAMILTON, ONTARIO
Workers are dwarfed by this enormous
storage vessel in the yard of this
Hamilton plant, where its building
required the skills of many millwrights,
welders, crane operators and engineers.

April 6, 1967

**SLATER STEEL
ELECTRIC FURNACE**
Slater Steel

HAMILTON, ONTARIO

The purpose of this assignment was to photograph a scrap bucket as it was charging the electric furnace at Slater Steel in Hamilton. One of the procedures in steel making, is to wait for the furnace heat cycle, in order to make the 'charge'. While waiting, I noticed another furnace about to pour its molten steel into a ladle. At a safe distance I climbed part way up a crane access ladder and watched. Not unlike a peak moment in sports photography, I had to expose when the pour was just right, without too much smoke. These images have been among my most used industrial photographs. They appeared in the company annual report and are symbolic of the Hamilton steel industry.

September 28, 1967

**STAINLESS STEEL
PRODUCTION**
Atlas Steels

TRACY, QUEBEC

Atlas Steels was the primary stainless and tool steel producer in Canada, exporting to world markets. One of the product applications was the CIBC Bank Tower in Toronto. This is the hot roll mill in Tracy, Quebec.

November 23, 1967

**CHURCH FURNITURE
MANUFACTURING**
Valley City Manufacturing

DUNDAS, ONTARIO
Founded in 1884, Valley City first entered
the woodworking business crafting
telephone boxes. The business evolved
into church, school, lab, courthouse, office
furniture and other specialty applications.
Portrayed in these photographs are
production and craftsmanship.

March 5, 1968

**UNDERWATER
SONAR EQUIPMENT**
Fleet Manufacturing

FORT ERIE, ONTARIO
Fleet Manufacturing in Fort Erie built
many interesting products, ranging
from complete small aircraft, to sections
of Boeing 747's, radar antennae and
naval sonar. These underwater sonar
components were a challenge to
photograph. Creative lighting and
camera angle was used to create
a bold representation.

March 21, 1968

RADAR ANTENNAE
Fleet Manufacturing

FORT ERIE, ONTARIO

As was the case in this era, interior of many of factories were old and not too attractive. After viewing my options, I arranged for an after-dark shoot of this large radar antenna, allowing me to light the product and eliminate background distraction. As large as this unit was, I needed minimal lighting. Because of the shape of the dish, light reflected like a mirror and simplified the lighting setup.

April 8, 1968

MOTOR GENERATOR DIVISION
Westinghouse Canada

HAMILTON, ONTARIO
On all industrial assignments, my main purpose was to show equipment, product and activity in an informative and positive way. Composition of the image is always paramount, and here, the addition of workmen in a realistic pose helps to define this large motor.

April 15, 1968

**WHAT'S INTERESTING
ABOUT THIS PHOTO?**
Firestone Tire

HAMILTON, ONTARIO
Firestone Stores were running a "brake
service special" advertising promotion.
I arranged with the police traffic control
to block off one lane at Hamilton's
busiest intersection at King & James,
at lunch hour. I crawled under the car
with my camera and signaled for the
pedestrian traffic to begin. A few staff
from R.T. Kelley advertising were added
to the pedestrian traffic across the
intersection at every light change, and I
was able to frame the under-carriage of
the car and emphasize the need to go to
Firestone for brake service.

April 15, 1968

**LARGE STEAM TURBINE
BEING SHIPPED**
Westinghouse Canada

HAMILTON, ONTARIO

Many of my assignment calls to Westinghouse Canada were on short notice and without much description as to what the subject would be. Upon arrival I learned that a large completely refurbished turbine was ready for shipment by rail. It could have been an very ordinary shot. I asked the foreman if we could re-sling the turbine and raise it a few feet above the flat car for the photograph. While this was being done I set up lights and camera, included the slinger for action and scale and made the exposure. It resulted in a large billboard and was used in local and national newspaper publicity.

September 1, 1968

**WESTINGHOUSE LARGE
MOTOR ASSEMBLY
(TURBO ALTERNATOR)**
Westinghouse Canada

HAMILTON, ONTARIO
Due to the large size of this motor
generator unit, the marrying of the two
components together and the extensive
quality control testing required, this
assembly was scheduled for a Sunday
morning. I had asked to be on the scene
before the multi-ton rotor was inserted
into the stator frame. I lit the equipment
to eliminate most of the background
to emphasize the equipment, then
directed the men and placement of the
rotor into position. I climbed inside the
stator frame to make the exposure.
This photograph appeared in newspapers
across Canada and won the Industrial
Photograph of the Year from a competition
of Canadian professional photographers.

September 6, 1968

TRAFFIC SAFETY SERIES
Ontario Ministry of Transport

BURLINGTON, ONTARIO
It was during summer holidays, so
for this series I corralled many of the
kids in my neighborhood to pose for a
simulated school safety scene.
I borrowed a school bus from a private
school for scenes to depict school bus
safety, then bicycle safety and other
themes in the series.

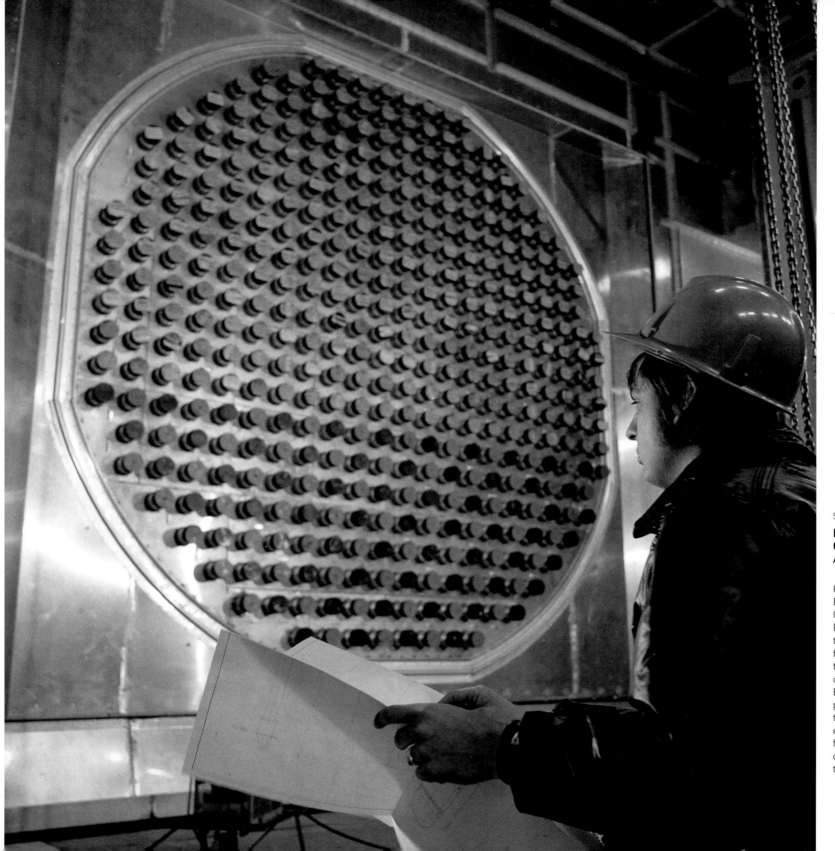

September 6, 1968

PICKERING REACTOR CONSTRUCTION
Atomic Energy of Canada

PICKERING, ONTARIO
During construction of the huge Nuclear Generating power plant complex at Pickering, I visited the site several times to produce informative images for media use. This reactor face shows the precision-built calandria fuel tubes, contrasted with a construction worker. Each fuel tube has a plastic cover for protection during construction. I missed the four letter word written on one of the end caps, even after making 50 copies for press releases. My client told me he corrected it before release, much to my relief.

December 14, 1968
**DOUGLAS POINT
NUCLEAR REACTOR**
Atomic Energy of Canada

TIVERTON, ONTARIO
The first operating Nuclear generating plant that I visited was the Douglas Point reactor. It was also the first of many site assignments for Atomic Energy of Canada over the next two decades. All of the photography that I produced for AECL was intended for media, so I selected subject areas that I could translate into simple, powerful images. You can imagine the complexity of some of the equipment in these massive plants.

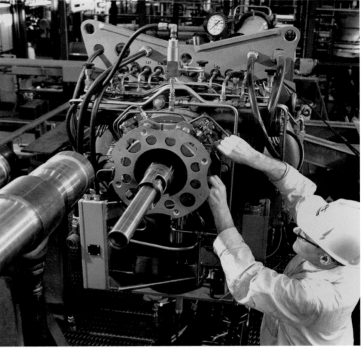

December 16, 1968

**AECL RESEARCH &
DEVELOPMENT LAB**
Atomic Energy of Canada

MISSISSAUGA, ONTARIO
At Atomic Energy's development labs
in Mississauga, projects for fuel handling
machines and other processes were
ongoing. Whenever I had the chance,
I used an unusual point of view
and positioning of technicians for
a strong composition.

July 23, 1969

TIRE BUILDING
Firestone Tire

HAMILTON, ONTARIO
This "earth-mover" tire really didn't look much like a tire in the early stage of construction. I used a low angle to exaggerate the size, and the carefully directed lighting to emphasize the detail.

February 13, 1969

TIRE INSPECTION QC LAB
Firestone Tire

HAMILTON, ONTARIO
Quality control is a factor of considerable importance in any industry. When I asked Firestone's lab technician lab if he had something representing destructive testing, there was nothing available. I asked for a sample that might show how serious they are about quality control. A section was cut out of a tire then analyzed, allowing me to visually communicate this message.

July 23, 1969

**DON MESSER & HIS ISLANDERS
WEEKLY TV SHOW**
CHCH Television

HAMILTON, ONTARIO

Don Messer and his Islanders videotaped weekly shows at CHCH-TV to the delight of many fans, featuring artists like The Buchta Dancers, Marg Osburne and Charlie Chamberlain.

July 23, 1969

DON MESSER & HIS ISLANDERS
WEEKLY TV SHOW
CHCH Television

HAMILTON, ONTARIO

This champion fiddler was one of the many celebrities that I met and photographed on regular shoots for CHCH-TV's Don Messer and His Islanders was a household name across Canada for many years.

September 3, 1969

RED CROSS BLOOD DONORS
United Appeal

BURLINGTON, ONTARIO

Ray Gentle was an advertising executive with whom I had worked for several years. He took on a pro bono project for the United Appeal, and asked me if I was interested in doing likewise. I said yes, as long as it wasn't cheque presentations. This series of editorial/PR photographs allowed me full freedom of content. The nurse immediately showed what a blood donation clinic was all about.

August 8, 1969

**ARC INDUSTRIES
TRAINING SESSION**
United Appeal

BURLINGTON, ONTARIO
This image of a student being taught
a meaningful task was one of a series
of photos for a publicity campaign for
the annual United Appeal. With a preconceived idea, I brought with me a
large sheet of glass, and a black cloth
to eliminate reflections. I carefully
instructed the models to achieve the
resulting photograph, which served
the campaign and also won second
place for North American-wide
United Appeal publicity.

March 6, 1969

MINIATURE GEAR SERVICE
Spar Aerospace

TORONTO, ONTARIO
Spar Aerospace is best-known for producing the world-famous Canadarm for space exploration. While on assignment at their Toronto facility, I noticed a technician carefully injecting a lubricant into a small gear case, and made this photograph of the unusual technique and application.

April 3, 1970

**A NEW BEER TANK,
CARLING BREWERY**
Atlas Steels

TORONTO, ONTARIO
Atlas Steels was Canada's largest
stainless & specialty steel maker with
a huge spectrum of applications for
their product. Stainless steel is difficult
to photograph at the best of times.
I opted to simplify my lighting, choose
an unusual perspective and place a
workman in a believable position inside
the tank for scale.

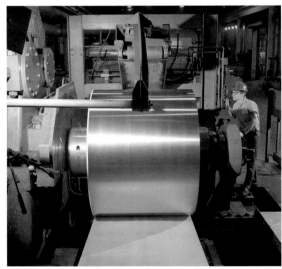

September 28, 1967

STAINLESS STEEL FINISHING
Atlas Steels

TRACY, QUEBEC

Think of steel mills and you might think of red hot steel and sparks everywhere. While there is a lot of that, some of the more challenging photographs show stages of production and finishing. The Atlas Steels mill in Quebec was built to produce architectural grade stainless steel in a variety of finishes for many domestic and international applications. Wherever possible I wanted to show functional processes in a unique way, so would occasionally utilize a pattern such as in the loop stainless steel in the continuous process.

September 20, 1961

CRUCIAL DECISIONS
Hamilton Tiger Cat Football Club

HAMILTON, ONTARIO
My many years of publicity photography
for the Ti-Cat football Team included
most home games. Here, Coach Jim
Trimble directs all-stars Bernie Faloney
(quarterback) and Hal Patterson
(receiver) at Hamilton Civic Stadium.
I enjoyed personal friendships with
many of the players.

September. 16, 1962

TIGER CATS IN ACTION
Hamilton Tiger Cat Football Club

HAMILTON, ONTARIO

In 1950 Ralph Sazio was a player on the first Tiger Cat Football Team, 12 years later he became one of the Team's most popular head coaches. John Barrow #61, Tim Reid #25 and Jim Whetham #12, confer with coach Sazio about game strategy.

The action on the field was exciting for the packed stadium.
Bobby Kuntz #23 was the ball carrier with blocking by #30 Bob Jeter.

February 27, 1981

**NEW PICKUP UNDERGOING
A QUALITY CONTROL CHECK**
Ford Motor Company of Canada

OAKVILLE, ONTARIO
Most of my photography assignments since 1956 evolved from referrals. Ford of Canada's annual report was one of many such accounts. Quality assurance is the highest priority in any company's image. This shot of end-of-line vehicle checkout training delivered a positive impression. (right) The automated welding robots performed precisely as the truck cabs were moved along the production line. Several exposures were made on the same film to achieve this.

April 6, 1967
'C' FURNACE
Slater Steel

HAMILTON, ONTARIO
A genuine respect for those who worked in industrial environments was critical to my safety and the safety of others. I would always observe a process before asking a subject to pose within the photographic composition. Patience and planning is also crucial. This electric furnace had been heating for several hours and tapping took only moments.

3
Transformers, turbines & a turtle

September 16, 1971
SUNSET VIEW
DOFASCO SKYLINE
Dofasco Steel

HAMILTON, ONTARIO
This was one of the most striking industrial sunsets I had ever seen.

I was on my way to photograph a dusk view, on speculation, of the Canadian Liquid Air plant in Hamilton, instead I saw the sky and clouds forming behind the Dofasco Bayfront plant. I stopped at my nearest opportunity on the shore of Hamilton Bay, setup my 4x5 camera and captured as many exposure of the scene before the light was gone. The resulting photograph was subsequently used by Dofasco for annual report and calendar and many times thereafter. I never did get the dusk shot of the Canadian Liquid Air plant.

"Light makes photography. Embrace light. Admire it. Love it. But above all, know light. Know it for all you are worth, and you will know the key to photography."

George Eastman, Kodak

As more versatility was required for location industrial photography, so too were the cameras and the portablility of electronic flash equipment.

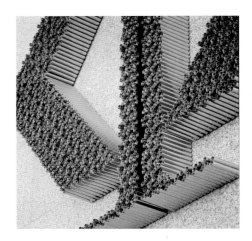

October 20, 1971

**STAINLESS STEEL
WINDOW FRAMES CIBC
COMMERCE COURT TOWER**
INCO

TORONTO, ONTARIO

The CIBC head office tower in Toronto would be the user of more stainless steel than any other Canadian structure, and my instructions were to show the components and applications in an innovative way.

At the manufacturer where the thousands of window frames were being built, I decided to squeeze into a corner for a different interpretation of my subject.

October 21, 1970

**SPECIALTY STEEL
COIN PUNCH**
Atlas Steels

ROYAL MINT, OTTAWA, ONTARIO
Showing specialty steels uses for Atlas
Steels allowed numerous opportunities
to photograph unique applications, this
time at Ottawa's Royal Mint. My task was
to illustrate the process of engraving the
master design for the punch. This began
as a large plaster cast, which was then
reduced using the old-fashioned
pantograph, to the actual size of the
1971 British Columbia centennial dollar.

The technician pours thousands of
newly minted quarters in the tote bin,
about $25,000.00 worth. Before entering
the production area, I was required to
remove my belt buckle and watch, empty
my pockets of keys, coins, pens or any
metallic object, and pass through a
metal scanner.

November 25, 1970

QUALITY CONTROL LAB
Firestone Tire

HAMILTON, ONTARIO
Test procedures were another aspect
of quality control for Firestone passenger
car tires. On occasions I photographed
in a department that used carbon black,
and would often end up with fine black
powder covering my body - and my
equipment. Clean up was a lot of work.

December 14, 1968

**DOUGLAS POINT
N!JCLEAR REACTOR**
AECL Atomic Energy of Canada

TIVERTON, ONTARIO
Although it was small in electrical
generating capacity, The Douglas Point
reactor on Lake Huron (Canada's first
Nuclear generating plant), was the
forerunner of the future mammoth
complexes. I had chosen the angle and
time of day to make this photograph but
the little tree left of centre was too tall.
I borrowed a wire coat hanger from the
guardhouse, secured the tree out-of-
frame and made the exposure.
The photograph became the most
widely used of this plant by Atomic
Energy of Canada.

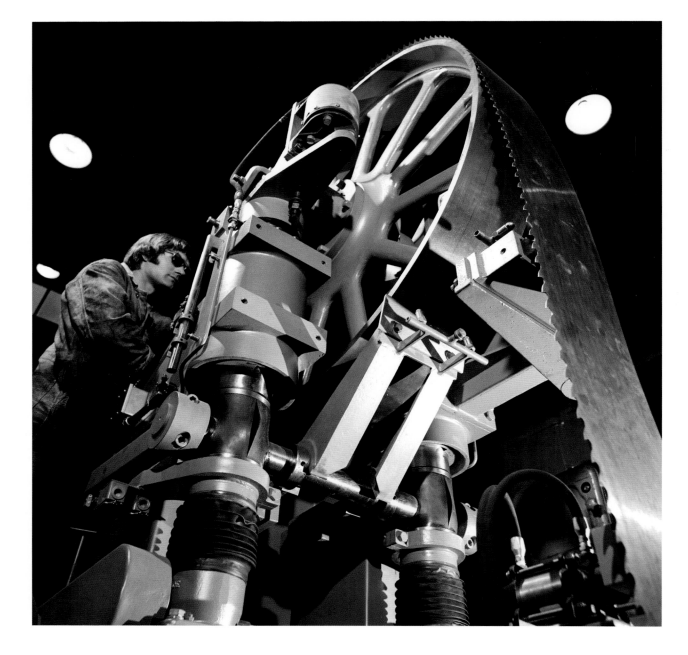

June 28, 1971

STAINLESS AND TOOL STEEL APPLICATIONS
Atlas Steels

VANCOUVER, BRITISH COLUMBIA

Before travelling, I would often inform a few clients of my schedule, so my assignments were often combined for economy of travel expenses. I attended a professional photographer's convention in Vancouver, and produced these subjects for Atlas Steels on this trip.

This documents a special application of tool steel on a large sawmill band-saw. Another interesting use of stainless steel was a protective grill for transport truck vertical mufflers. Unless the product itself was aesthetically pleasing or self-explanatory, I almost always included people in the photograph for scale and human interest.

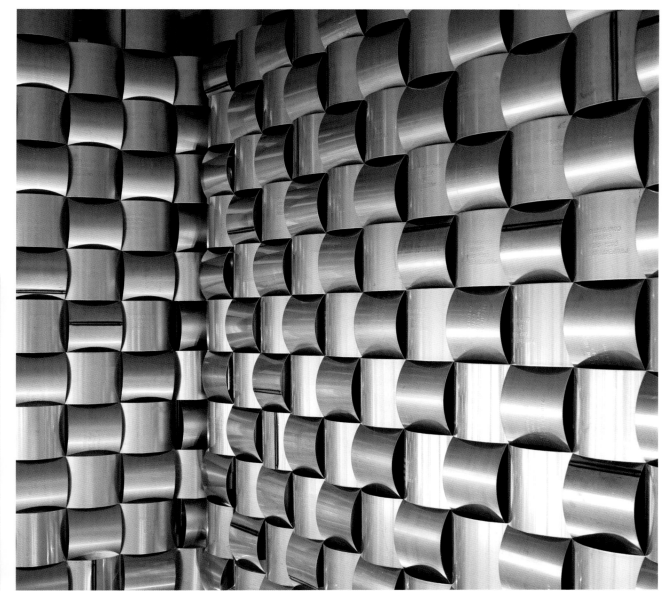

July 24, 1971

STAINLESS STEEL KEGS
INCO International Nickel Co.

WOODSTOCK, ONTARIO

Firestone made more than tires. Firestone Steel in Woodstock, Ontario manufactured stainless steel beer and beverage containers. I photographed these in various stages of fabrication. Rather than shooting a solitary object, patterns are a good photographic alternative that make visual interest more dynamic.

August 19, 1971

RAIL CAR PAINT DRYING BOOTH
National Steel Car

HAMILTON, ONTARIO
The company's new owner needed some dramatic images of plant products and manufacturing. By placing the silhouetted man in the foreground, I created depth in this paint-drying tunnel.

March 24, 1984

STAINLESS STEEL BEARING
Slater Steel

CHARLESVILLE, PENNSYLVANIA
Slater Steel's Ft. Wayne, Indiana plant produced stainless steel bearings for nuclear submarines.

Seeing that the bearings became completely blackened from the heat-treating process, I opted to photograph them before they were processed. The resulting image was used on the annual report cover.

November 15, 1971

**LARGE TRANSFORMER
AT SHIPPING DOCK**
Westinghouse Canada

HAMILTON, ONTARIO
On a cold, dull November day, a photograph
of a transformer waiting to be shipped
didn't seem too exciting. By using the life-
saving buoy as a frame, the image became
very graphic.

December 16, 1971

STONE CUTTING SAW
Steetley Industries

QUEENSTON, ONTARIO
As a segment of a multi company
annual report, I photographed this large
Queenston quarry stone block being
cut to size by an enormous diamond-
tipped saw. Industrial sites such as this
are usually damp and dirty but setting
lights strategically can make the
process graphically informative.

December 16, 1971

PUBLICITY FOR NEW
THEATRE AUDITORIUM

HAMILTON, ONTARIO
To promote publicity for the new
theatre and aid in fundraising, a couple
of professional ballet dancers provided
a pleasant contrast to a stark
construction site.

(Below) Boris Brott, the Hamilton
Philharmonic conductor sits
in the soon-to-be auditorium
of Hamilton Place.

March 18, 1972

PYRAMID WALL
Hamilton Place

HAMILTON, ONTARIO
While Hamilton's theatre auditorium
was under construction, several publicity
photographs were needed. At the site,
I noticed the unusual pattern created
by the bricks, which had been specially
formed to enhance acoustical qualities
of the theatre. This brick wall pyramid
design can be recognized by anyone
who has enjoyed a concert in the
Great Hall of Hamilton Place theatre.
I added additional lighting from the
second balcony to create this dramatic
photograph that won an architectural
photo award.

April 15, 1972

DR. RONALD J. GILLESPIE , C.M.
PROFESSOR OF CHEMISTRY
F.R.S., F.R.S.C., F.R.S.C.(U.K.), F.C.I.C
McMaster University

HAMILTON, ONTARIO
I made hundreds of publicity photographs
of the many aspects of McMaster, and
personality profiles were an important
focus of a growing university. Dr. Ronald
Gillespie was head of the chemistry
department and over the years has
become one of the world's leading
experts in developing the Valence Shell
Electron Pair Repulsion (VSEPR) model
of molecular geometry.

Fifteen years after this photograph was
made, I was invited by Dr. Gillespie and
Dr. David Humphreys to produce 125
photographs of teaching experiments for
a university level chemistry book. This
was the first time a North American
chemistry textbook was printed in
colour. Two later versions were also
produced adding some newer images.

June 10, 1972

FROST FENCE DIVISION
Stelco Steel Company of Canada

ROCKTON, ONTARIO
The Frost Fence division of Stelco
needed a visual representation of their
chain link product. At Rockton African
Lion Safari I was escorted by a park
ranger in a pickup truck to the lion and
tiger section. The truck side window
was opened for the photography and
we needed to be fairly close. Needless
to say, the cheetah (the world's fastest
land animal) and I were both nervous.

June 15, 1972

**HEAT TREATMENT
OF SPECIAL STEEL ALLOY
IN VACUUM FURNACE**
Atlas Steels

WELLAND, ONTARIO
Getting into hot spots was quite a
regular occurrence for me. When
metals are heat-treated to achieve
certain molecular qualities, there are
several processes involving oil, brine, air
or vacuum. These heating and cooling
cycles must be precisely controlled.

Though visually there was considerable
light emitting from these steel rods,
additional lighting was needed to define
the elements of the photograph. On
occasion, my lighting equipment has
melted because of being too close, too
long. Timing is always important for
this type of photography.

June 27, 1972

GEAR CASES
Bridge & Tank Co. Ltd.

HAMILTON, ONTARIO
The St. Lawrence Seaway project provided considerable manufacturing work for the Bridge and Tank Company. These gear cases were part of the many mechanisms used in waterway locks and gates. Almost always, I included a workman in the shot to present the subject in proper perspective.

August 19, 1972

TURTLE CROSSING ROAD

THOROLD, ONTARIO
Returning from one of many assignments
in the Niagara Peninsula, I captured this
frame of a turtle crossing the busy
highway. The Hamilton Spectator
published the photo the next day.
Payment was $10.

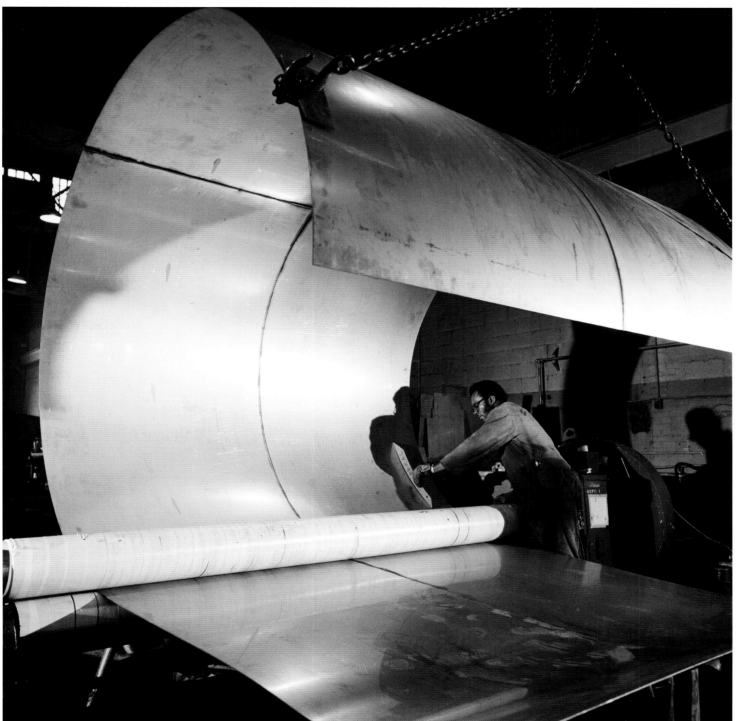

September 7, 1972

BEDARD TANK TRAILER
Atlas Steels

MONTREAL, QUEBEC
In this application, stainless steel was being formed for a highway tanker trailer. Shapes are enhanced by angle and lighting, so too is the potential for the photograph to be used effectively.

September 26, 1972

DC-AC HIGH VOLTAGE
AECL Atomic Energy of Canada

DORSEY RECTIFIER STATION, MANITOBA
One of my assignments for Atomic
Energy of Canada took me to this
electricity conversion station, near
Winnipeg. The Dorsey Station was
designed to convert high voltage
DC (direct current) from Nelson River
Power on Hudson Bay, to 60 cycle
AC (alternating current) for distribution
into the Manitoba grid.
The unusual apparatus made for
challenging photography.

October 18, 1972

WESTINGHOUSE APPLIANCES
Westinghouse Canada

HAMILTON, ONTARIO
Appliances are mass-produced by the thousands. This is a preparation stage for the "box" of an electric clothes dryer, which would then be chemically cleaned and painted. The angle suggests productivity and volume. Showing the man through the opening helps to emphasize the pattern.

October 12, 1972

CHEMISTRY RESEARCH
National Research Council

OTTAWA, ONTARIO

McMaster University was a major client for public relations photography. One of their partnerships was with the National Research Centre in Ottawa. McMaster was asked to provide photographs of an electron microscope used at the University. NRC was impressed with the quality of my photography and black and white prints, and invited me to Ottawa for a two-day shoot in their Chemistry Research Department.

November 10, 1972

NEW #3 BLOOM & BILLET MILL
STELCO Steel Company of Canada

HAMILTON, ONTARIO
#3 Bloom & Billet Mill at Stelco had recently been brought on-line, and their soaking pit (ingot reheating) for hot rolling was a multi-million dollar expansion. The company needed to show the facilities to shareholders while they still looked new. As each ingot of steel approached the mill I needed to time my exposure to catch the full process, and the effect caused by the glowing steel.

January 15, 1973

**STEAM TURBINE ROTOR
QUALITY CONTROL CHECK OF
TURBINE ROTOR ASSEMBLY**
Westinghouse Canada

HAMILTON, ONTARIO
Gas and steam turbines are complex
machines, and require exacting
tolerances at every stage of assembly
because they run at very high rpm's.
Having become somewhat familiar with
many aspects of turbine production, I
was always looking for new opportunities
to view these components in a meaningful and dramatic way. The position of
the technician was important for visual
dynamics of this image, but it had to be
technically correct, and safe as well.

January 18, 1973

**POWER TRANSFORMER
MANUFACTURING**
Westinghouse Canada

HAMILTON, ONTARIO
Here, the workmen give an indication
of scale in this transformer photo that
was taken from high above the subject
from a traveling bridge crane. On one
occasion I was shooting from atop a
large transformer like this. Still using
flash bulbs to light large areas, I was
inserting the bulb into the flashgun.
The bulb ignited with my fingers
wrapped around it, severely blistering
all of my right hand. Needless to say it
was painful. I climbed down the ladder
and went to first aid for treatment.
Half an hour later, my hand bandaged
up, I completed the photograph.

January 18, 1973

**POWDERED METALLURGY
PROCESS**
INCO / Grace Company

ST. THOMAS, ONTARIO
This was the first occasion that I had
seen a process using metal powders.
I shot these auto transmission gears
in the various steps of manufacture at
the plant. The gears are formed under
great pressure, then heat-treated and
have perfect finish with no further work
required. In comparison, cast products
would require many more stages of
machining, grinding, time and expense.
I conceived a simulated condition that
would convey heating, and show some of
the shapes of these high tech automotive
transmission gears, using some of the
powders in this studio illustration. The
photograph appeared on the cover of
the Inco News magazine.

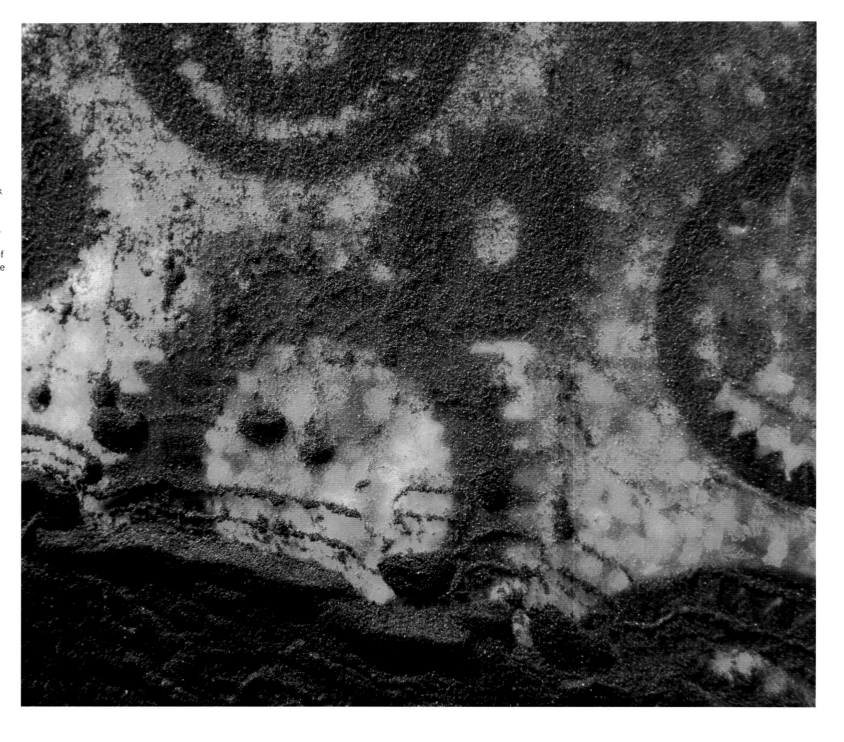

March 27, 1973

HEAVY EQUIPMENT
THERMAL BOILER FABRICATION
Foster Wheeler Company

ST. CATHARINES, ONTARIO

Virtually all metalworking and fabricating plants generate a considerable amount of dust, dirt and oil fumes. The less clutter and pollution that is apparent, the better the company image. Lighting, composition and command of the scene help to create a 3 dimensional perspective. The power plant boiler section was setup for this image and the exaggerated viewpoint shows the scale of the equipment.

April 24, 1973

$500,000 SPIRAL STAIRCASE
INCO

TORONTO, ONTARIO
It was described to me as a "half million dollar staircase" and I tried to show the stainless steel and glass design as effectively as possible. I was on a seven-day assignment to present a diversity of stainless steel architectural applications for a multi-page brochure. The publication listed every supplier to the then-new CIBC Commerce Court Tower in Toronto.

July 1, 1973

ROTARY SUMMER CAMP
Rotary Club of Hamilton

HAMILTON, ONTARIO
Some of my favourite photographs
are those that I initiated upon seeing
a window of opportunity. When I took
my family on a Sunday car trip to the
Rotary Easter Seals summer camp on
Lake Erie, I had it in mind to capture
an interesting image to describe the
Rotary motto 'service above self'. This
photograph conveyed the elements of
need, empathy and Rotarian service.
It became a feature photograph in the
Rotary International Year Book in 1974.

April 30, 1974

SLATER STEEL
Bridge & Tank

HAMILTON, ONTARIO
This "cooling bed" is exactly that - a
large area for reinforcing bar (rebar) to
cool after forming from a red hot billet.
The bars leaving the roll forming mill at a
speed of 10 kph and can be precarious for a
person standing nearby. I was fortunate
to have left my vantage point a minute
before the red hot bars broke through
the safety barrier and 'cobelled' at the
end of the cooling bed.

The control room operator maneuvers
the billets in the sizing mill and on the
cooling table.

September 19, 1973

**PICKERING NUCLEAR
POWER PLANT**
Atomic Energy of Canada

PICKERING, ONTARIO
The first thought when looking at this
nuclear reactor photograph would be to
assume it was taken from a boat – not
so. As with all the nuclear plants in
Canada, I was required to shoot aerial
photography, this one with the aid of a
skilled helicopter pilot.

After photographing from several
angles, I asked him to fly just over
the water. He did, in a swooping pass,
achieving one of the most-used views of
the Pickering Nuclear Generating Station.

April 15, 1974

**MODEL OF GENTILLY II
NUCLEAR POWER REACTOR**
Atomic Energy of Canada

MISSISSAUGUA, ONTARIO
The new design of the 600 megawatt
nuclear reactor was created initially in
the form of a scaled size Plexiglas model.
For a cover story in Ascent magazine,
I placed coloured lighting inside the
structure to emphasize the silhouetted
technicians in the foreground.

April 30, 1974

SPAR AEROSPACE
GEAR MANUFACTURING
Spar Aerospace

TORONTO, ONTARIO
Famous for the Canadarm in space, Spar Aerospace also refurbished helicopter rotor gearboxes. To produced this image of gear assembly, I used a multiprism lens and coloured light.

I wasn't aware that the image had ever been used until I saw it on the cover of a metalworking magazine while sitting in an office lobby.

4

Salt mines,
cheese makers
& 'nickel pigs'

May 15, 1970

**WELLAND CANAL
CONSTRUCTION**
Red-D-Mix Concrete

THOROLD, ONTARIO

"Never boss people around. It's more important to click with people than to click the shutter."

Alfred Eisenstaedt, photo journalist, Life Magazine

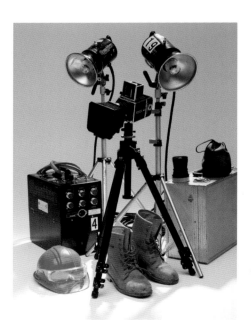

With advances in techniques and skills, more lighting capacity, cameras and lenses were required. Safety on the job was a priority.

May 15, 1970

**WELLAND CANAL
CONSTRUCTION**
Red-D-Mix Concrete

THOROLD, ONTARIO
This major expansion project for
re-routing the Welland Canal between
Lake Ontario and Lake Erie required
thousands of cubic yards of concrete to
be trucked from the batching plant in
on a continuous time line. The image
was used in an annual report.

December 11,1970

PAPER MILL
Stewart-Hinan Construction

THOROLD, ONTARIO
The newly completed paper production
line was part of a massive installation.
The contractor wanted to show an
example of their versatility.

August 12, 1974

INTO THE SALT MINES UNDER LAKE HURON
Knockler-Moeller

GODERICH, ONTARIO
Being asked to photograph electrical equipment in a salt mine was not quite what I had expected. I descended from the ground level in a mine hoist crew cage. The depth of the working area of the Goderich salt mine was 1750 feet, but the actual mining area extended two miles horizontally under Lake Huron. I was transported throughout the cavernous area in a crew truck similar to a vehicle used above ground. The salt was mined with heavy earth-moving equipment that had been brought below in pieces and re-assembled. Conveyor systems moved the salt through the mine to crusher and screening machines, and the salt was then taken to the surface to be used as road salt and water softeners.

October 24, 1974

PLANT FIRE
Halliday Homes Manufacturing

BURLINGTON, ONTARIO
I was in Burlington photographing a personal injury accident scene near the Joseph Brant Memorial Hospital, when I noticed clouds of black smoke a few blocks to the west of the hospital. I drove toward the smoke to discover that the Halliday Homes factory and mill were on fire. Normally, I wouldn't have stayed near the scene, but decided to make some exposures of the spectacular fire. I also met the Hamilton Spectator photographer who was covering the fire.

When I returned to the studio I received a phone call from the photographer. He had a problem with his camera and wanted to see what I had shot. I quickly processed the film and one of my photos was used on the front page of the newspaper.

July 16, 1975

CASTING OPERATIONS
Fahralloy Metals

ORILLIA, ONTARIO
This metal casting plant produced a variety
of cast components. These photographs
show molten metal being poured into a
mold, forming a long, continuous chain,
one link at a time.

May 3, 1976

**ALGOMA STEEL
CRANE TROLLEY**
Bridge & Tank

HAMILTON, ONTARIO
One of my assignments at this company was to show some of the massive products that were produced. A crane trolley in excess of 20 tons was being readied for shipment to Algoma Steel in Sault Ste. Marie. With a lift of this magnitude not a lot of photographic control can be exercised. Finding an angle which included the workmen gave a dramatic perspective.

July 7, 1976

OPEN PIT MINE SITE
Indusmin Ltd.

NEPTHON, ONTARIO
Another new experience for me was
to photograph the various processes
at this open pit mine. The production
stages included blasting the rock at the
mine site, crushing and pulverizing and
then extracting nepheline syenite for
paint and ceramic applications.

July 6, 1976

OPEN PIT MINE
Indusmin Ltd.

CANUTE, QUEBEC
Rock drillers were preparing for a series of blast holes on the rim of the open pit mine, which was then detonated in sequence to effectively dislodge and break up the ore from the face of this quarry wall. It was then trucked to the crusher and separated to extract minerals such as silica.

(top) Tom on location.

October 10, 1976

NICKEL MINING OPERATIONS
INCO

THOMPSON, MANITOBA

INCO's 1975 annual report required images of the mine site at Thompson, Manitoba. I photographed the production and mining of nickel ore, and ore being brought to the conveyor that transports it to the processing plant. In the image on the left, the mine head is framed by a hydro tower, and a colour filter was used to emphasize the sunset. The lighting on the truck came from my rental car.

October 20, 1976

MILE DEEP INCO NICKEL MINE
INCO

SUDBURY, ONTARIO
I had studied the work of other industrial photographers for mining, and tried to visualize what I might achieve for the 1976 Inco Annual Report. Because the location was a mile below ground level, I wanted to be prepared with any equipment I might need. The area I selected was a stope which was being prepared with a ceiling safety grid. I then placed the miners in a realistic position with technical and safety input from the mine expert who was my guide. Carrying a lot of lighting equipment to this area wasn't very practical so I opted to use ol' fashioned flashbulbs, which I fired by remote control to create this silhouette. I felt very good about this shot, which took a while to execute and didn't feel that we needed more views. When we reached the top, it suddenly struck me, 'were the miners wearing their safety glasses?' To my relief, my guide assured me, 'yes'. In my concern for all the aspects of a classic mining shot, a mistake here would have been drastic.

November 15, 1976

**COKE OVEN
FURNACE CHARGING**
Dofasco

HAMILTON, ONTARIO

Production of coke is the burning off of gas and tar from coal - a key element in steel making. At this Dofasco coking furnace, the lid is removed to recharge the furnace with coal from the top. Wearing the necessary safety equipment in a potentially dangerous place was an important aspect of recording this dramatic scene.

November 15, 1976

ANNUAL REPORT PHOTOGRAPHY PLANT OPERATIONS
Dofasco

HAMILTON, ONTARIO

No matter how large an industrial plant is, it is important to present the facility to be dramatic, functional and interesting. These views highlight the magnitude and scope of the steel industry. Glowing steel ingots radiate intense heat even as they are cooling. The modern cold roll mill prepares the steel for another stage toward final applications.

November 16, 1976

BEACHVILLE LIME PLANT
Dofasco

BEACHVILLE, ONTARIO
For Dofasco's 1976 annual report, I
needed one representative photograph of
their Beachville Lime plant at Ingersoll.
To emphasize the quarry and plant's 24
hour operations, a dusk view also hides
some of the less photogenic aspects of
a sprawling plant. The facility processed
calcium limestone, used mainly as a
flux in the steel making process.

December 29, 1977

BAYCOAT STEEL COATING PLANT
Baycoat (Dofasco / Stelco)

HAMILTON, ONTARIO
A joint venture of Dofasco and Stelco, Baycoat produces coated and pre-painted steel for appliances, automotive, homes, barns and other use. Special equipment processed the coils in various colours, profiles and textures. This viewpoint was selected to create a dynamic view of the finishing operation. The photograph was taken for Dofasco's 1976 Annual Report.

October 20, 1977

**SUNRISE - PICKERING
NUCLEAR REACTOR**
Atomic Energy of Canada

PICKERING, ONTARIO
This was one of the few photographs
that just - happened. I was traveling
to the Peterborough area to do aerial
photography of an open pit mining
operation. My 5:00 a.m. start would
normally have me arriving at the ideal
time but as I drove toward that area,
dense fog started to roll in. I decided
to cancel and return home. On the
way back, I noticed the sun was just
rising behind the Pickering Nuclear
Generating Power Plant, and gave me
an opportunity to capture an unsolicited,
environment friendly, classic image.
I showed this image to my client at
AECL, and they decided it would be
great for a brochure cover and an
enlarged mural in their Ottawa head
office lobby. Sometimes it's great to
have 'best laid plans go astray'.

November 3, 1977

PORT COLBORNE
NICKEL PROCESSING PLANT
INCO

PORT COLBOURNE, ONTARIO
At Port Colborne, Inco processed
cobalt "buttons" and nickel "pigs". This
compelling image shows the end of the
smelter process as the molten nickel is
poured in small molds called 'pigs'.

July 12, 1978

REACTOR FUEL BUNDLE MANUFACTURING
Westinghouse Canada

PORT HOPE, ONTARIO
Over the years, I was fortunate to be assigned to photograph all of the nuclear power generating plants across Canada and also many equipment manufacturers and research facilities. At the Westinghouse Canada Nuclear Products plant in Port Hope, I photographed the making of the fuel bundles for the Candu Reactor. These are precision built and filled with enriched Uranium 32.

As I packed up my equipment after a day-long shooting session throughout this plant, I noticed these finished fuel bundles ready for crating. I asked a quality control person to pose for this last shot of the day. It was used worldwide in newspapers, brochures and posters.

September 27, 1978

HEAVY WATER PROCESSING PLANT
Atomic Energy of Canada

GLACE BAY, NOVA SCOTIA
Heavy water (deuterium oxide) is a very expensive moderating product used in the Candu Nuclear Reactor. AECL had two of these plants, including this one in Glace Bay, NS.

Most of the exterior apparatus and structure at these plants is not very interesting in daylight, often due to distracting clutter. Making a dramatic dusk image can enhance the location.

The plant's intricate control room gives an indication of the complex process of making Heavy Water.

October 1, 1978

NUCLEAR RESEARCH FACILITY
Atomic Energy of Canada

WHITESHELL-PINEWA, MANITOBA

For a segment in a special series of photographs, I travelled to the Nuclear Research facility at Pinewa, MB.

In the 'hot cell' area (radiation sensitive) the technicians remotely manipulate the handling of radioactive materials through protective walls. As part of the entry and departure at the 'hot cell area', my equipment and my clothes had to be checked for any radiation contamination, sometimes requiring more than one pass to clean any contamination. Specialized chemical analysis is another aspect of this research facility.

October 15, 1978

NUCLEAR REACTOR FUELLING TUBE PREPARATION
Atomic Energy of Canada

PT. LEPREAU, NEW BRUNSWICK
Atomic Energy of Canada (AECL)
continued to build domestic nuclear
power plants, and I had many
opportunities to photograph various
aspects of equipment installations.
Pt. LePreau, for New Brunswick Power,
was the last major Candu reactor
built in Canada.

Technicians work on this 650 megawatt
calandria which is the heart of the
reactor. Fuel bundles are inserted
into all of these tubes and the area
becomes completely radioactive when
the reactor is powered up.

October 15, 1978

**NUCLEAR POWER PLANT
STEAM TURBINE**
Atomic Energy of Canada

PT. LEPREAU, NEW BRUNSWICK
A central component of the generating
process in a power plant, whether fossil
fuel, oil, gas or nuclear, is the steam
turbine which turns the generators
that produce the electricity. The size
of these turbines is enormous and,
when running, spin at very high speeds.
Before the containment enclosure
housing is placed over thousands of
turbine blades, a technician inspects
some of the clearances and final
housekeeping in the area.

October 21, 1978

**LA PRADA
HEAVY WATER PLANT**
Atomic Energy of Canada

GENTILLY, QUEBEC

This heavy water (deuterium oxide) production plant in Gentilly, QC was one of several that were planned for construction in Canada. Technology in the production of heavy water improved so rapidly that this and others were mothballed and never completed.

September 19, 1979

RAIL TANK CAR REFURBISHING
Babcock Wilcox Refractories

TRURO, NOVA SCOTIA
A whirlwind two-day assignment for
Babcock Wilcox Refractories took me
to Magog, QC to photograph brick kilns,
and then to this rail tank car refurbishing
location in Truro, NS. A series of ruptures
caused potential environmental concerns,
and the tank cars were refurbished with
'Kawool' high temperature insulation.
The car in the background is covered with
insulation, waiting for the steel skin to be
moved and welded into place.

September 11, 1979

NATURAL GAS PROCESSING
Consumers Gas

CARSTAIRS & BRAGG CREEK, ALBERTA

I was sent to Calgary and surrounding areas for the Consumers Gas Annual Report to photograph their subsidiary, Home Oil, at Carstairs, AB. I depicted various segments of the company's operations. A by-product of natural gas is sulphur. Removed from the gas in a liquid state, sulphur solidifies as it is exposed to air. It was amazing to see a 10 metre high, 20 x 30 metre storage pile.

September 11, 1979

NATURAL GAS DRILLING
Consumers Gas

TURNER VALLEY, ALBERTA
Turner Valley, AB was one of the first
major natural gas finds in Canada and
continued as a major producer for many
years. The driller construction platform
was completely self-contained and a
portable village supplied the crews with
goods and accommodations. I can attest
that the meals were fabulous.

October 29, 1980

**SPIDER WEB
REBAR INSTALLATION**
Atomic Energy of Canada

TIVERTON, ONTARIO
Nuclear plant construction is an
expensive and lengthy process, involving
years of design, engineering and
coordination of numerous components.
The purpose of one of my visits to the
Bruce "B" Nuclear Generating plant
site at Tiverton was to interpret many
aspects of construction progress.

Rebar (reinforcing bar) being webbed is
an essential component of solid
concrete construction. The challenge
was to create images that show ordinary
situations in a new and interesting light.

October 30, 1980

**NUCLEAR VACUUM
SAFETY BUILDING**
Atomic Energy of Canada

PICKERING, ONTARIO
One of the important safety features
of the Candu Nuclear Reactor is the
Vacuum Building. The upper portion
of this special concrete structure is a
reservoir for millions of liters of water.
In the event of a nuclear radiation
emergency within any of four reactors,
the contaminated air is sucked from
the reactor through cavernous concrete
ducts into the vacuum building. Millions
of liters of water are then sprayed down
to isolate and neutralize any radiation
until the problem is repaired.

This occasion was a media tour
promoting the safety aspects of the
Candu Heavy Water Reactor design.
After the tour I made this dramatic
view with the aid of a technician.

December 2, 1980

DE LAVAL CHEESE MACHINE
Atlas Steel

PETERBOROUGH, ONTARIO
It seems there is no end to stainless
steel applications, especially in the food
industry, or to the different grades of
stainless steel. This image shows the
paddle system, part of an enormous
cheddar cheese processing machine
under construction at the De Laval
equipment plant.

February 27, 1981

**BABCOCK WILCOX
BOILER MANUFACTURING**
Atomic Energy of Canada

CAMBRIDGE, ONTARIO
AECL- Babcock Wilcox in Cambridge
ON, manufactured some of the large
components used for nuclear and
thermal power generation. On my many
visits to industrial fabricating plants, I
always looked for elements of interest
and design. In this image the crane
operator is guiding the boiler segment
through the plant.

February 20, 1981

LADLE PREPARATION
Inland Refractories

NANTICOKE, ONTARIO
The Stelco Lake Erie plant is a new mill
built on the shore of Lake Erie which
produces steel with a modern continual
casting operation. The aim of this
photograph was to show the oxygen
lances (to the right of the ladle). These
refractory materials sustain intense
heat and allow them to be inserted
into the ladle and oxygen is used to
separate the impurities of the steel
making process.

March 19, 1982

MINE SCOOP IN OPERATION
Jarvis Clark Manufacturing

CALEDONIA, ONTARIO

Ore handling requires very special equipment. The scoop tram is a powerful large capacity machine designed for low ceiling height mines.

To photograph this equipment and location, I used a "painting with portable flash lighting" technique. My assistant (son Jean-Pierre) directed the flash lighting at specific areas and with varying intensity to help me to create a realistic scene. Since this method requires up to eight exposures on one frame of film, everything must be totally dark during the exposures. The machine's lights and helmet lamps were turned on for only a few seconds at the end of the exposure. The operator remained motionless.

August 22, 1982

**NIGHT AERIAL VIEW
FLAMBORO RACEWAY**
Flamboro Downs

DUNDAS, ONTARIO

The first Confederation Cup Standard Bred Championship Race was set to go on this August 1982 Civic Holiday weekend at Flamboro Downs. I had been asked by the owners to record this momentous event. Along with photographing many aspects of track activities, I was challenged to provide an aerial view at dusk. Film speeds had to be push processed to 800 ASA, (not available off the shelf) in order to photograph at this time of day and minimize movement from the helicopter. I boarded the helicopter in a field near the track and timed our short flight to coincide with the start of the race at the critical time for dusk photography. Our photographing distance from the track had to be appropriate not to spook the horses. If I didn't get the shot during this 2 minute race I would have missed the 'window' of evening light.

September 21, 1982

WATER PROCESSING VESSELS
Glegg Water Systems

BURLINGTON, ONTARIO
Any equipment can be glamourized
if appropriate techniques are used.
Lighting, angle and worker position
all contribute to the effectiveness of
the composition. This water treatment
system was being tested before crating
and shipment.

5

Fuelling tubes, microchips & Slowpokes.

October 14, 1997

AUTOMATED ROLLING MILL
Algoma Steel

SAULT STE. MARIE, ONTARIO

This photograph (and hundreds more) evolved from a former advertising agency receptionist. A 5 pm telephone call from Fran, with whom I had not been in touch with for at least 20 years, "Did I still do industrial photography?" Her recommendation resulted in several photographic trips to Algoma Steel in Sault Ste. Marie. In this image I was attempting to catch the red hot steel strip going through new the mill. Complex adjustments to the equipment were needed, but it finally worked.

"Without the opportunity there is no photograph."

Tom Bochsler

Film use gradually disappeared as digital technology forged ahead. Scanning of images was replaced by direct digital camera files and enhanced software and computers.

September 29, 1982

PETRO-CHEMICAL REACTOR
Union Carbide

SARNIA, ONTARIO
Annual reports for this company
required more than just a photograph.
Some insight was required to convey
the corporate message at this chemical
processing plant. This chemical reactor
tower at Union Carbide, was newly
constructed and promised an increase
in productivity and efficiency. The
golden colour at dusk enhanced this
composition dramatically.

September 29, 1982

HEAVY DUTY PRESSURE VESSEL COMPONENTS
Guelph Engineering & Manufacturing

GUELPH, ONTARIO
Large industrial items have many stages of fabrication. The key to a good interpretation of a subject is to select the optimum stage of manufacture, move the components if possible, and choose the best angle, composition and lighting.

October 28, 1982

**TRAVELLING BRIDGE CRANE
AIR CANADA**
Secord Manufacturing

TORONTO, ONTARIO
This 120-foot crane spans the image area from end to end of the maintenance hanger, shared by a mammoth Jumbo Jet 747. The image suggests function and scale.

In the Secord Manufacturing plant (right), a high capacity crane undergoes final inspection before knock down and shipment.

October 14, 1982
TURBINE HALL
Atomic Energy of Canada
New Brunswick Power

PT. LEPREAU, NEW BRUNSWICK
After the steam is produced from the
nuclear reactor, it is forced through a
series of pipes to the turbine hall where
massive turbines turn the generator to
produce the electricity.

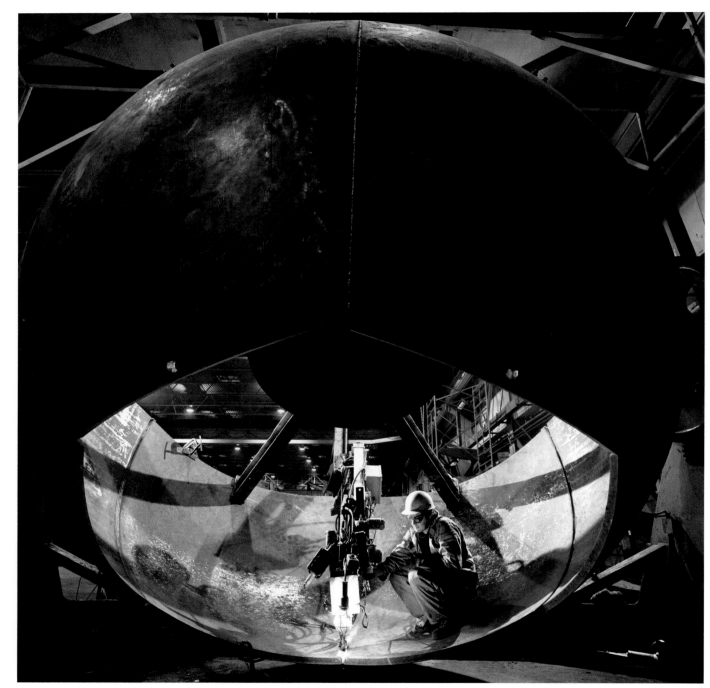

January 10, 1983

SPACE SHIP
Canadian Lukens Company

TORONTO, ONTARIO
This year we decided to promote our
photography at an industrial products
trade show, displaying large prints of a
variety of our work that we were doing.
Not much business was generated by
the trade show visitors, but another
exhibitor at the show liked what we did
and that's how this assignment evolved.
The company, Canadian Lukens Ltd.
built very complex large steel vessels.
I selected this viewpoint to emphasize
the size, and create some drama.

May 13, 1983

**LCBO PACKAGE
HANDLING SYSTEM**
Jervis B. Webb Mfg.

HAMILTON, ONTARIO

Material handling equipment is not necessarily glamorous, but this line-up of automated package handling units for a Liquor Control Board of Ontario warehouse displayed many positive features of the company's capabilities.

Various stages of fabricating show the complexity of the equipment.

April 5, 1983

THE GREAT WALL
Personal Work

BEIJING, CHINA

I helped to organize a trip of 5 professional photographers, which evolved into a 3 week visit and lecture tour of parts of China. In 1983, caucasians were a novelty unseen in certain parts of China. We caused quite an attraction wherever we went. One hotel (a walled compound) was vacant when we arrived for an overnight stay. The next day, the compound was filled with hundreds who came to see us as we were leaving.

May 12, 1983

AUTOMATED EGG COLLECTION SYSTEM
Martindale Hatchery

CAYUGA, ONTARIO
Most of us accept day to day items without thinking, "Where does it come from?", "How is it made?" I had never seen high volume poultry production until I was asked to visit this chick hatchery. I photographed the many aspects of the operations including automated egg collection (direct from the laying pens), grading and packaging.

May 13, 1983

**LOGGING SKIDDER
OPERATIONS**
Timberjack

CHARLESVILLE, PENNSYLVANIA
Timberjack was the dream of two
men in Woodstock, Ontario and their
prototype logging skidder pulled logs
out of the bush, previously done by mules
and horses. Their company developed
into a major employer and exported
the Timberjack skidder all over the
world. My photography for the company
encompassed many years of interesting
assignments in Northern Ontario, New
Brunswick, Pennsylvania, and more.
Showing the power and productivity of
the Timberjack was always important,
but the photos also had to imply safety
and environmental sensitivity.
(not running over small trees.)

April 2, 1985

TIMBERJACK SKIDDER
Timberjack Limited

WOODSTOCK, ONTARIO
The plant assembly line for forestry skidders required timing and co-ordination of personnel. Production interruptions had to be kept at a minimum. This image was used for trade publications, advertising and press releases. Good housekeeping also suggested good safety standards and was a prerequisite in all of my industry photographs.

January 19, 1984

THOMAS A. EDISON MUSEUM
AECL Ascent Magazine

FORT MYERS, FLORIDA
As part of a picture story for Ascent Magazine, I was sent to the Edison Museum at Fort Myers, Florida. The original lab had all the elements and atmosphere of the era when Edison perfected the electric light bulb. I asked the tour guide to find a lab coat to help me depict an early Edison research technician, so he borrowed this coat from his chiropractor.

January 19, 1984

THOMAS A. EDISON MUSEUM
AECL - Ascent Magazine

FORT MYERS, FLORIDA

At the Edison Museum in Fort Myers there were an amazing array of inventions, 1093 to be exact, that Thomas Alva Edison had patented. He built a summer residence next to the homes of Henry Ford and Harvey Firestone.

My sighting of the 8 inch bust of Edison on a shelf in a closet gave me an idea to double expose his original electric light bulb with a silhouette of the bust.

July 23, 1984

SCIENCE NORTH MUSEUM
AECL Ascent Magazine

SUDBURY, ONTARIO
A favourite photograph of mine was
this dusk shot of the Science North
Museum in Sudbury. This is the last
photo that I made on a day-long series
of activities throughout the museum.
The photo story depicted the interaction
of the educational friendly exhibits.
Having completed most of the series
I scouted a location for this shot.
I returned at the appropriate time,
prepared for everything - camera,
film, light meter, but not for mosquitoes.
I was wearing a short sleeved shirt
and the mosquitoes were ferocious.
I couldn't stop shooting because the
sky pattern and the light were fast
disappearing. It proved well worth the
pain. Not only did this appear on the
cover of Ascent magazine and a poster
for Science North, but the architect
Raymond Moriyama saw the photograph
and ordered copies for several years.

September 17, 1984

NUCLEAR REACTOR
Atomic Energy of Canada

PT. LEPREAU, NEW BRUNSWICK
This daylight view is my most requested photograph, more than 20 years later. I photographed all of the Nuclear Generating Plants in Canada over a period of several years. Pt. Lepreau, was one of the latest reactors built. After spending two days photographing interior and aerial photographs, I needed a ground level overall view of the complex. By including a few wild flowers and the reflecting water it became a classic. I also returned that evening to achieve a dramatic night view.

September 17, 1984

SPENT FUEL BAY
AECL Ascent Magazine

PT. LEPREAU, NEW BRUNSWICK
The spent fuel bay was a safety
containment area for depleted uranium
fuel bundles which were removed from
the reactor, then stored under water to
confine radiation until permanent
storage was available. It being a potential
contamination area, I wore a complete
protective suit and had to place booties
on my tripod as well. Then everything
had to be checked and clear of
contamination on my way out of
that zone.

September 17, 1984

TURBINE HALL
AECL Atomic Energy of Canada

PT. LEPREAU, NEW BRUNSWICK

For the layperson, it is hard to visualize what a nuclear power plant would look like. This image graphically shows the turbine hall, where steam that is produced by the nuclear reactor, is forced into the massive turbines to generate electricity. My perspective with the crane hook in the foreground and the technician, relates to the size of the complex.

October 16, 1984

**REACTOR FUELLING TUBE
MANUFACTURING**
Westinghouse Canada
Nuclear Products

COBOURG, ONTARIO
Westinghouse was in the forefront of
producing supplies and components
for the Canadian Nuclear industry. At
their manufacturing plant in Cobourg,
Zirconium fueling tubes for the reactor
calandria and fuel bundle rods are
made with precision.

December 19, 1984

**MICROCHIP VERIFICATION
- QC AUTOMATIC TESTING**
Linear Technology (Gennum Corp.)

BURLINGTON, ONTARIO
In 1984 I was commissioned by a
specialty manufacturing company,
Linear Technology of Burlington, ON
(now called Gennum Corp.) to photograph
various stages of production of hearing
aid microchip circuitry.

This automated circuit tester identifies
any flawed circuits at very high speed.
Rejects can be discarded.

July 10, 1985

DR. AUBREY CRICH
ORAL SURGEON/PHOTOGRAPHER
AECL - Ascent Magazine

GRIMSBY, ONTARIO
Dr. Crich was an oral surgeon whose passionate hobby was photography of nature, flowers and insects. Using some of the most basic 35mm camera equipment and a lot of patience, his skills became world famous. Part of his collection was obtained by the Ontario Science Centre. A delightful man, I photographed him for a magazine story. His personality and love of photography shows clearly in my portraits.

October 1, 1986

GAS FLAME
Union Gas Limited

TORONTO, ONTARIO
The annual report for Union Gas required
a symbolic cover shot. I conceived this
image by photographing the reflection
of a Bunsen burner gas flame into three
stainless steel cylinders in a darkened
room. Simple, but effective. A logo and
other graphics were added.

May 5, 1986

**DOWNTOWN BURLINGTON
NIGHT VIEW**
City of Burlington

BURLINGTON, ONTARIO
While creating a series of photographs
in a high rise apartment building, I
chose the roof of the building to show
the view on a very clear evening. This
rewarding Lake Ontario shoreline scene
has been my most requested photograph
of downtown Burlington.

May 02, 1995

WATER TREATMENT
Zenon Environmental Inc.

BURLINGTON, ONTARIO
This was an assignment for a shot
of advanced clean water technology
equipment. Realizing that there were
some very interesting components I
chose some lighting effects, design and
included the technician to enhance this
factory assembly.

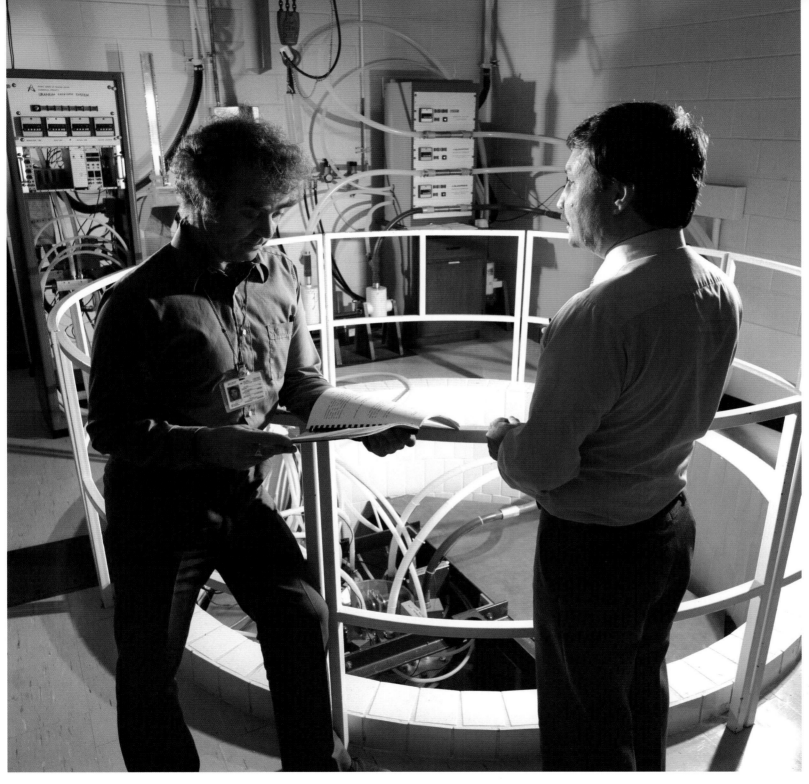

March 4, 1986

SLOWPOKE NUCLEAR REACTOR
Atomic Energy of Canada
Nordion Division

ROYAL MILITARY COLLEGE OF CANADA
KINGSTON, ONTARIO
The 'slowpoke' nuclear reactor was installed at the research facility of Queen's University, Kingston, ON.

My assignment was to show it effectively. Because it was built below ground level, I showed some of the components and used coloured lighting. With the operator and technician in the foreground, the image became 3-dimensional.

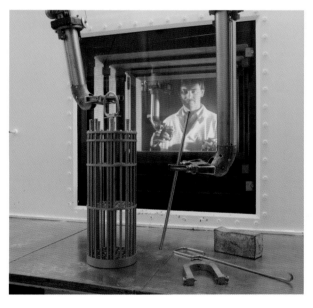

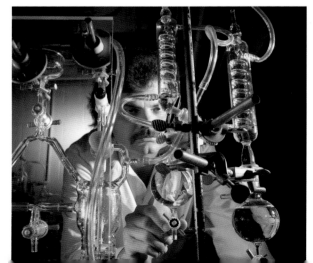

March 4, 1986

ISOTOPE PRODUCTION
AECL - Nordion Division

KANATA, ONTARIO

I had many occasions to visit the Nordion Plant in Kanata to document the activities of this commercial nuclear isotope production facility. As is apparent in the images, considerable care is taken to insure safety of technicians. This environment required that I be dressed accordingly and was equipped with a monitor which records accumulated radiation levels. I was then able to go into most of the critical areas to cover this assignment effectively.

April 24, 1986

TURBINE COMPONENT
MACHINING
Westinghouse Canada

HAMILTON, ONTARIO
Annual reports have always been
a challenge to photographers as
management usually dictates a theme,
whether for capital expenditures,
technology, capability, employees
or shareholders benefits. This theme
illustrated several aspects of expertise,
efficiency and technology in turbine
manufacturing for Westinghouse
Canada's 1988 annual report.

April 11, 1989

TOM & BOB
Slater Industries

SOREL, QUEBEC
Our assignment was to photograph a high capacity 400 ton press in operation, at what used to be a cannon barrel manufacturing plant in Sorel, QC. Bob Chambers, a long time friend and photographer was with me on this trip. We provided the client with a fine image of their press. We still disagree as to who's idea it was to shoot the portraits of us in action in the old foundry with streaming sunbeams.

September 25, 1991

**AERIAL BRUCE NUCLEAR
GENERATING STATION**
AECL Atomic Energy Canada

TIVERTON, ONTARIO
In 1969, I became the photographer of
record for Atomic Energy of Canada
public relations. Aerials always
presented an overview. Whenever I
chartered a Cessna 172 aircraft,
I would routinely do a preflight check
and remove a small screw from a
latch, so that I could fully open the
side window. This time I didn't check,
and had to direct the pilot to tip the
plane at an angle as we flew past
the reactor site, to allow me to shoot
through an eight inch opening.

September 25, 1991

PAPER MILL OPERATIONS
Canadian Pacific Forest Products

THUNDER BAY, ONTARIO
Referrals are our best and most
rewarding source of business.
This assignment was referred by a
photographer who felt the requirement
was beyond his capability, (one of the
benefits of belonging to a professional
photographers association).

My assignment was an intensive two
day photo shoot at the Canadian Pacific
Forest Products operations in Thunder
Bay, including helicopter photographs
of Canada's largest paper mills.
The finishing end-of-line provided a
dramatic graphic view of the facility and
appeared in the national media.

December 2, 1992

NEW OFFICE TOWER
Canada Trust

KITCHENER, ONTARIO
The newest Canada Trust office building
in downtown Kitchener was a very
interesting building architecturally. On
this cold December day I gained access
to an old four storey building across the
street, where the flat roof happened to
be somewhat icy. I waited for the ideal
time at early evening light and, with
some traffic to cause streaks in the
street during the long exposure.

The main lobby was very graphic and
the art director volunteered to stand in
the shot for scale.

December 3, 1992

METRO CENTRE TORONTO, WAVE CEILING DESIGN
Canadian Gypsum Company

TORONTO, ONTARIO
The Canadian Gypsum Company has a division dedicated to ceiling design applications. Although this photograph doesn't look like a ceiling in the usual sense, it was a specialty application which I photographed at the Metro Centre in Toronto. My choice of angle, composition and time of evening, dramatized the product application so much that it was used in the company's international annual report.

February 17, 1994

BAXTER PHARMACEUTICAL WATER TREATMENT
Zenon Environmental Inc.

ALLISTON, ONTARIO
This world-renowned water treatment equipment manufacturer built some unique products. This one was installed at a pharmaceutical company in Alliston. I arrived mid-morning and photographed various internal components, but I perceived an opportunity to do something special. It was almost lunch time and the construction crew in this area left for their break. Since this glassed-in room was jutting out on the second floor, I commandeered the power lift platform, had the light turned off outside the room, then I positioned the technician and made the photograph.

September 26, 1994

CASTLE KILBRIDE
Ventin Group Architects

BADEN, ONTARIO

James Livingston known as the flax mill king, built this stately historical home in 1877. It was restored as a museum and attached to the new municipal offices for the Township of Wilmot in central Ontario. My series of images focused on these rooms and many other features to convey the character of this heritage building.

April 12,1995

LASER ALIGNMENT
S.McNally & Son

TORONTO, ONTARIO
A major expansion at the Metro
Toronto Convention Centre required
a connection between other buildings
in the complex. This 103 meter by 3.7
meter horseshoe service tunnel was built
with precise accuracy using the laser.

Working in this environment meant
being dressed for the conditions,
including rubber boots.

October 1, 1997

THE LEARNING CURVE
Ventin Group Architects

CAMBRIDGE, ONTARIO

Architectural photography has always appealed to me, and as part of a series of interior and exterior images, I needed a good overall view of St. Benedict Catholic High School. Usually sunlight and shadows help make the exterior views three dimensional. Not in this case. It was starting to rain. I selected the angle with the running track in the foreground and later through the medium of digital imaging added a complementary sky. It was the most requested image for this multi use secondary school complex.

April 05, 1987

TERRACOTA WARRIORS
Personal Work

XIAN, CHINA

My son Peter (designer of this book) joined me on my second trip to China. We were fortunate to visit Xian and the Terra-cotta Warrior exhibit of hundreds of life sized figures. Photography was strictly prohibited inside the building but with a little ingenuity I was able to capture this image by cradling my camera under my arm and with a little guessing for composition, looked away from any scrutinizing eyes, and clicked.

September 14, 1984

**POPE JOHN PAUL II
VISIT TO TORONTO**
The Hamilton Spectator

TORONTO, ONTARIO

When Pope John Paul II visited Canada, The Hamilton Spectator asked if I would assist their photographers to cover yet another vantage point of the visit at Nathan Philips Square at Toronto City Hall. I was assigned to a pre-selected room on the 18th floor of Sheraton Four Seasons which gave a great viewpoint. Security was very tight so I setup my cameras and tripod near the window which could easily be seen by the roof top security around the Square.

My wife Doreen joined me to see the scene below and shortly before the Pope was due to arrive there was a knock on the door. Two RCMP and hotel security had been notified of our presence by the roof top spotters. They made a cursory look around our room and as they were leaving said that we had a better view than their command centre below. I made many exposures with wide and telephoto lenses of the Pope and the crowds. Several were published in the next edition of the Hamilton Spectator.

June 6, 2003

JUNO BEACH CENTRE
Juno Beach Association

COURSEULLES-SUR-MER, FRANCE
An opportunity presented itself to me to photograph the Canadian designed Juno Beach Centre Memorial in France. I was delighted to be at the official opening and photograph the architectural features and the emotional event.

Designed by Burlington architect Brian Chamberlain, the museum honours Canadian forces.

I had no media credentials for the opening day, but I was able to convince the protocol staff that I had a valid reason to have freedom of movement for photographing the international dignitaries at the ceremonies.

June 6, 2003

CANADIAN WAR CEMETERY
Personal Work

BERNYS-SUR-MER, FRANCE

On a very special visit to Juno Beach Centre, I was accompanied by my wife Doreen and daughters, Cindy and Marianne. We were deeply moved by the sacrifice that was displayed by Canadians at nearby Bernys-sur-mer.

Acknowledgements

Since the early 1950's I have been fortunate to have clients who became true friends, and have recommended my skills to others. Being entrusted to interpret the subject before me, and to communicate it both visually and graphically has been my goal throughout my career.

Descriptions of the photographs throughout this collection are intended to engage your interest, not about film, lenses and exposure, but of some of the challenges and experiences involved in making the photographs.

In 2006, I was pleased to exhibit a series of my industrial and event photographs at the Art Gallery of Hamilton. Many of the same images now appear in this book. It was one of their most successfully attended exhibitions with more than a thousand visitors.

To those who have offered encouragement over these many years since I began assembling the images and writing the text, I offer my sincere gratitude.

A special thanks to my son Peter, for his graphic and creative talent in designing this book, and to my co-workers at Bochsler Creative Solutions and BPImaging.

I have accumulated almost a million photographs which have now become a part of Canadian history. I have donated my collection to Library and Archives Canada (Ottawa), and the Hamilton Public Library.

Thanks to Mark Zelinski, my publisher. Without his experience and motivation I might still be procrastinating.